W9-CDK-850

What people are saying about
Inside a U.S. Embassy . . .

I am absolutely a fan of this book. What makes it so interesting is that it's about individuals and what they do, and it's about how they support the United States in an active way.

> MARC GROSSMAN
> *Career Ambassador & Under Secretary of State for Political Affairs*

Every day in hundreds of places around the world, thousands of your fellow Americans are at work in direct support of you and your interests. From helping Americans in trouble, to formulating American foreign policy, to talking to foreign leaders about cooperation in hundreds of different areas from trade and technology to preventing nuclear war, these people make a difference. This book tells the fascinating inside story of how it all works.

> THOMAS R. PICKERING
> *Boeing Company Senior Vice President for International Relations*
> *and former Under Secretary of State for Political Affairs*

Inside a U.S. Embassy is required reading for the first week of my university seminar on practical diplomacy. My students are amazed at the variety and uniqueness of Foreign Service work described in the book's first-hand accounts. I wouldn't teach the course without it.

> GENTA HAWKINS HOLMES
> *Ambassador & Diplomat in Residence, University of California, Davis*

Inside a U.S. Embassy sits on my desk and I recommend it to all interested in the Foreign Service.

> KARL F. INDERFURTH
> *Professorial Lecturer at George Washington University's Elliott School of International Affairs,*
> *and former Assistant Secretary of State for South Asian Affairs*

Readers will find an up-to-date, compelling, interesting, accurate and highly readable depiction of the Foreign Service and its vital role in service to our nation. The profiles and the stories all show the rich diversity of our people, in terms of both their varied backgrounds and the wide range of services they perform.

> RUTH A. DAVIS
> *Distinguished Advisor for International Affairs at Howard University*
> *and former Director General of the Foreign Service*

An anthology of brief essays and personal testimonies penned by experienced professionals. . . . includes profiles . . . typical days . . . and amazing glimpses of the Foreign Service in action during moments of crisis. A fascinating revelation of the tireless men and women who labor to represent America abroad.

> *Midwest Book Review*

INSIDE A
U.S. EMBASSY

HOW THE
FOREIGN SERVICE WORKS
FOR AMERICA

INSIDE A
U.S. EMBASSY

HOW THE
FOREIGN SERVICE WORKS
FOR AMERICA

Updated and revised for 2005.

Editor and Project Director: Shawn Dorman

Project Advisor: Susan Reardon

Associate Editors: Kelly Adams-Smith, Steve Honley, Susan Maitra

Art and Design Director: Caryn Suko Smith

Editorial and Research Assistants: Marc Goldberg, Mikkela Thompson

Reader: Dick Thompson

Interns: Sarah Martin, Christina O'Hara, Stephen Yeater

Cover Artist: Connie McLennan

With special thanks to the individual Foreign Service contributors and
to the members of the Inside Embassy Advisory Committee:
Kelly Adams-Smith, Louise Crane, Ambassador Willard De Pree, Perri Greene,
Ambassador William Harrop, Steve Honley, Lisa Kierans, Susan Maitra, Niels Marquardt, John Naland,
Susan Reardon, Mikkela Thompson, Ward Thompson, and James Yorke.

American Foreign Service Association
Washington, D.C.

American Foreign Service Association

2101 E Street N.W.

Washington, DC 20037

(202) 338-4045; (800) 704-2372

www.afsa.org

Copyright © 1995, 2003, 2005 by the American Foreign Service Association

All rights reserved.

First Edition, 1995, edited by Karen Krebsbach

Second Edition, 2003, edited by Shawn Dorman

Second Edition, Second Printing, 2005, edited by Shawn Dorman

ISBN 0-9649488-2-6

Library of Congress Control Number: 2002117840

Source for profile section maps: The World Factbook, 2002

For information on ordering additional copies of this book, go to www.afsa.org/inside, e-mail embassybook@afsa.org, or call 1 (800) 704-2372. Discounts available for quantity orders.

~

DEDICATED TO
THE MEN AND WOMEN OF THE
U.S. FOREIGN SERVICE.

~

Table of Contents

Part 2

**A Day in the Life of the Foreign Service: One-Day Journals from
Embassy Staff around the World** **56**

Part 3
The Foreign Service in Action: Tales from the Field

Why This Book?

BY SHAWN DORMAN

Many Americans do not know what the Foreign Service is or understand what goes on inside a U.S. embassy. Yet the work done at our embassies and consulates around the world by the people who make up the Foreign Service is vitally important to America — our security, our economy, and our democracy. Every day consular officers help stranded Americans get home. Every day economic and commercial officers assist U.S. businesses to compete overseas. During times of upheaval, political officers are the ones on the front lines keeping Washington informed about the real situation. U.S. diplomats negotiate the international agreements that end the wars, keep the peace, and protect and promote U.S. interests. Foreign Service diplomats and specialists are truly the unsung heroes of American foreign policy.

This book will give you an up-close and personal look into the work and lives of the people who make up the United States Foreign Service. The people you will meet work at big embassies as well as tiny consulates, in Asia, Africa, Europe, Latin America, and the Middle East. They are ambassadors and they are junior officers. They are development professionals, press officers, and computer experts. They are a diverse group, but they all share the same mission — to serve their country.

In the Profile section, meet Foreign Service employees in each type of position in a typical U.S. embassy and gain a sense of the key role played by each member of an embassy team. In the Day in the Life section, take a rare hour-by-hour look at what Foreign Service employees actually do on the job, in Kabul and in Vladivostok and elsewhere.

The final section — Tales from the Field — gives you a sense of the extraordinary. Look behind the scenes of some historic events. See how the Foreign Service meets the challenges of today's complex world: the threat of terrorism, the coups, the civil wars, the natural and not-so-natural disasters, and the evacuations.

So come on inside ...

What Is the Foreign Service?

BY JOHN W. LIMBERT AND JOHN K. NALAND

The 13,000 men and women of the Foreign Service represent the government and people of the United States. At over 250 diplomatic and consular posts, the U.S. Foreign Service safeguards national security and manages America's relationships with the rest of the world. America's diplomacy began in the eighteenth century with Benjamin Franklin, Thomas Jefferson, John Adams, and others, dispatched abroad by the young nation to promote its vital interests. Thanks to their skilled diplomacy, the warring colonies received the vital French help that finally turned the tide of the revolution. In the years that followed, separate diplomatic and consular services evolved, each staffed mostly by short-term appointees who changed en masse after each new president took office.

Efforts to replace this inefficient "spoils system" intensified after President Theodore Roosevelt issued a 1906 order that began to de-politicize the consular service and after President William Howard Taft issued a 1909 order to modernize the diplomatic service. Then, responding to America's increasing foreign involvement during and after World War I, Representative John Jacob Rogers (R-Mass.) sponsored legislation to unify the diplomatic and consular services into a single corps of professionals recruited and promoted on the basis of merit. The Foreign Service Act of 1924, known as the Rogers Act, established a career Foreign Service to serve the president as a skilled corps of professionals who possess understanding of the affairs, cultures, and languages of other countries and who are available to serve anywhere in the world. The Rogers Act of 1924 and the Foreign Service Act of 1980 remain the cornerstones of today's Foreign Service.

At any given time, about two-thirds of Foreign Service personnel work at our embassies and consulates abroad — serving one- to three-year tours — and one-third work in the United States, mostly in Washington, D.C. Overseas, they are assisted by 30,000 Foreign Service National (local) employees. Domestically, they work beside Civil Service colleagues who provide continuity and expertise in functions such as legal, consular, financial, and cultural affairs. Foreign Service members work in five federal agencies: the State Department, the U.S. Agency for International Development, the Department of Commerce's Foreign Commercial Service, the Department of Agriculture's Foreign Agricultural Service, and the International Broadcasting Bureau (primarily at the Voice of America). Foreign Service members may serve tours at other U.S. government agencies, including the National Security Council, the Office of the U.S. Trade Representative, and the Department of Defense. They also hold positions at universities, in private companies, and on congressional staffs.

The Foreign Service is a career like no other. It is much more than a job; it is a uniquely demanding and rewarding way of life. As representatives of the United States to foreign governments, Foreign Service members have a direct impact on people's lives and witness history in the making. They work alongside highly talented colleagues and face the unexpected every day, in situations that push their ingenuity and creativity to the limit.

But a Foreign Service career also imposes significant demands. Typically, Foreign Service members spend two-thirds of their careers overseas, sometimes in unhealthy or isolated locations. They live for extended periods of time far from parents, siblings, and old friends, and sometimes without familiar amenities or modern medical facilities. Due to increasing international terrorism, Foreign Service members face physical danger and may be required to serve an "unaccompanied" tour or to remain at their duty posts in harm's way after their families are evacuated. Over 150 Foreign Service men and women, for example, are serving their country in Iraq under conditions of unprecedented danger.

Most Foreign Service veterans, however, have found that the rewards of representing our nation far outweigh the personal burdens. Diplomacy is an instrument of national power, essential for maintaining effective international relationships, and a principal means through which the U.S. defends its interests and responds to crises. The Foreign Service is a proud profession, safeguarding American interests by: managing diplomatic relations with other countries and international institutions; promoting peace and stability in regions of vital interest; bringing nations together to address global challenges; promoting democracy and human rights around the world; opening markets abroad to create jobs at home; helping developing nations establish stable economic environments; helping ensure that American businesspeople have a level playing field on which to compete; protecting U.S. borders and helping legitimate foreign travelers; and assisting U.S. citizens who travel or live abroad.

The American Foreign Service Association helps the Foreign Service in this vital work. Established in 1924 — the same year as the Foreign Service itself — AFSA is both a professional association and the collective bargaining representative for all active and retired Foreign Service professionals, over 23,000 people. It negotiates the regulations affecting employees' careers, advocates Foreign Service issues before Congress, and communicates its professional concerns to the news media and general public. AFSA works to make the Foreign Service a better supported, more respected, and more satisfying place to spend a career and raise a family. These goals, in turn, serve to make the Foreign Service an even more effective agent of U.S. international leadership.

— John W. Limbert and John K. Naland served as AFSA presidents,
from 2003 to 2005 and 2001 to 2003, respectively.

U.S. Presence in

AFGHANISTAN
   Kabul (E)
ALBANIA
   Tirana (E)
ALGERIA
   Algiers (E)
ANDORRA
   Andorra la Vella (-)
ANGOLA
   Luanda (E)
ANTIGUA & BARBUDA
   St. Johns (-)
ARGENTINA
   Buenos Aires (E)
ARMENIA
   Yerevan (E)
AUSTRALIA
   Canberra (E)
   Melbourne (CG)
   Perth (CG)
   Sydney (CG)
AUSTRIA
   Vienna (E)(M)
AZERBAIJAN
   Baku (E)
BAHAMAS
   Nassau (E)
BAHRAIN
   Manama (E)
BANGLADESH
   Dhaka (E)
BARBADOS
   Bridgetown (E)
BELARUS
   Minsk (E)
BELGIUM
   Brussels (E)(M)
BELIZE
   Belize City (E)
BENIN
   Cotonou (E)
BERMUDA
   Hamilton (CG)
BHUTAN
   Thimpu (-)
BOLIVIA
   La Paz (E)
BOSNIA & HERZEGOVINA
   Sarajevo (E)
   Banja Luka (BO)
   Mostar (BO)
BOTSWANA
   Gaborone (E)
BRAZIL
   Brasilia (E)
   Rio de Janeiro (CG)
   Sao Paulo (CG)
   Recife (C)
BRUNEI
   Bandar Seri Begawan
   (E)
BULGARIA
   Sofia (E)

BURKINA FASO
   Ouagadougou (E)
BURMA
   Rangoon (E)
BURUNDI
   Bujumbura (E)
CAMBODIA
   Phnom Penh (E)
CAMEROON
   Yaounde (E)
CANADA
   Ottawa (E)
   Calgary (CG)
   Halifax (CG)
   Montreal (CG)(M)
   Quebec (E)
   Toronto (CG)
   Vancouver (CG)
CAPE VERDE
   Praia (E)
CENTRAL AFRICAN
REPUBLIC
   Bangui (E)
CHAD
   N'Djamena (E)
CHILE
   Santiago (E)
CHINA
   Beijing (E)
   Chengdu (CG)
   Guangzhou (CG)
   Hong Kong (CG)
   Shanghai (CG)
   Shenyang (CG)
COLOMBIA
   Bogota (E)
COMOROS
   Moroni (-)
CONGO, DEMOCRATIC
REPUBLIC OF THE
   Kinshasa (E)
CONGO, THE REPUBLIC OF
   Brazzaville (E)
COSTA RICA
   San Jose (E)
COTE D'IVOIRE
   Abidjan (E)
CROATIA
   Zagreb (E)
CUBA
   Havana (IS)
CYPRUS
   Nicosia (E)
CZECH REPUBLIC
   Prague (E)
DENMARK
   Copenhagen (E)
DJIBOUTI
   Djibouti (E)
DOMINICA
   Roseau (-)
DOMINICAN REPUBLIC
   Santo Domingo (E)

EAST TIMOR
   Dili (E)
ECUADOR
   Quito (E)
   Guayaquil (CG)
EGYPT
   Cairo (E)
EL SALVADOR
   San Salvador (E)
EQUATORIAL GUINEA
   Malabo (E)
ERITREA
   Asmara (E)
ESTONIA
   Tallinn (E)
ETHIOPIA
   Addis Ababa (E)
FIJI
   Suva (E)
FINLAND
   Helsinki (E)
FRANCE
   Paris (E) (M)
   Marseille (CG)
   Strasbourg (CG)
GABON
   Libreville (E)
THE GAMBIA
   Banjul (E)
GEORGIA
   Tbilisi (E)
GERMANY
   Berlin (E)
   Dusseldorf (CG)
   Frankfurt (CG)
   Hamburg (CG)
   Leipzig (CG)
   Munich (CG)
GHANA
   Accra (E)
GREECE
   Athens (E)
   Thessaloniki (CG)
GRENADA
   St. George's (E)
GUATEMALA
   Guatemala City (E)
GUINEA
   Conakry (E)
GUINEA-BISSAU
   Bissau (-)
GUYANA
   Georgetown (E)
HAITI
   Port-au-Prince (E)
HOLY SEE
   Vatican City (E)
HONDURAS
   Tegucigalpa (E)
HUNGARY
   Budapest (E)
ICELAND
   Reykjavik (E)

INDIA
   New Delhi (E)
   Calcutta (CG)
   Chennai (CG)
   Mumbai (CG)
INDONESIA
   Jakarta (E)
   Surabaya (CG)
IRAN
   Tehran (-)
IRAQ
   Baghdad (E)
IRELAND
   Dublin (E)
ISRAEL
   Tel Aviv (E)
   Jerusalem (CG)
ITALY
   Rome (E) (M)
   Florence (CG)
   Milan (CG)
   Naples (CG)
JAMAICA
   Kingston (E)
JAPAN
   Tokyo (E)
   Naha, Okinawa (CG)
   Osaka-Kobe (CG)
   Sapporo (CG)
   Fukuoka (C)
   Nagoya (C)
JORDAN
   Amman (E)
KAZAKHSTAN
   Almaty (E)
   Astana (BO)
KENYA
   Nairobi (E) (M)
KIRBATI
   Tarawa (-)
KOREA, NORTH
   P'yongyang (-)
KOREA, SOUTH
   Seoul (E)
KUWAIT
   Kuwait (E)
KYRGYZSTAN
   Bishkek (E)
LAOS
   Vientiane (E)
LATVIA
   Riga (E)
LEBANON
   Beirut (E)
LESOTHO
   Maseru (E)
LIBERIA
   Monrovia (E)
LIBYA
   Tripoli (E)
LIECHTENSTEIN
   Vaduz (-)
LITHUANIA
   Vilnius (E)

LUXEMBOURG
  Luxembourg (E)
MACEDONIA
  Skopje (E)
MADAGASCAR
  Antananarivo (E)
MALAWI
  Lilongwe (E)
MALAYSIA
  Kuala Lumpur (E)
MALDIVES
  Male (-)
MALI
  Bamako (E)
MALTA
  Valletta (E)
MARSHALL ISLANDS
  Majuro (E)
MAURITANIA
  Nouakchott (E)
MAURITIUS
  Port Louis (E)
MEXICO
  Mexico City (E)
  Ciudad Juarez (CG)
  Guadalajara (CG)
  Monterrey (CG)
  Tijuana (CG)
  Hermosillo (C)
  Matamoros (C)
  Merida (C)
  Nogales (C)
  Nuevo Laredo (C)
MICRONESIA, FEDERATED
STATES OF
  Kolonia (E)
MOLDOVA
  Chisinau (E)
MONACO
  Monaco (-)
MONGOLIA
  Ulaanbaatar (E)
MOROCCO
  Rabat (E)
  Casablanca (CG)
MOZAMBIQUE
  Maputo (E)
NAMIBIA
  Windhoek (E)
NAURU
  Yaren (-)
NEPAL
  Kathmandu (E)
NETHERLANDS
  The Hague (E)
  Amsterdam (CG)
NETHERLANDS ANTILLES
  Curacao (CG)
NEW ZEALAND
  Wellington (E)
  Auckland (CG)
NICARAGUA
  Managua (E)

NIGER
  Niamey (E)
NIGERIA
  Abuja (E)
  Lagos (CG)
NORWAY
  Oslo (E)
OMAN
  Muscat (E)
PAKISTAN
  Islamabad (E)
  Karachi (CG)
  Lahore (C)
  Peshawar (C)
PALAU
  Koror (E)
PANAMA
  Panama City (E)
PARAGUAY
  Asuncion (E)
PAPUA NEW GUINEA
  Port Moresby (E)
PERU
  Lima (E)
PHILIPPINES
  Manila (E)
POLAND
  Warsaw (E)
  Krakow (CG)
PORTUGAL
  Lisbon (E)
  Ponta Delgada, Azores
  (C)
QATAR
  Doha (E)
ROMANIA
  Bucharest (E)
  Cluj-Napoca (BO)
RUSSIA
  Moscow (E)
  St. Petersburg (CG)
  Vladivostok (CG)
  Yekaterinburg (CG)
RWANDA
  Kigali (E)
SAINT KITTS AND NEVIS
  Basseterre (-)
SAINT LUCIA
  Castries (-)
SAINT VINCENT AND THE
GRENADINES
  Kingstown (-)
SAMOA
  Apia (E)
SAN MARINO
  San Marino (-)
SAO TOME AND PRINCIPE
  Sao Tome (-)
SAUDI ARABIA
  Riyadh (E)
  Dhahran (CG)
  Jeddah (CG)
SENEGAL
  Dakar (E)

SERBIA & MONTENEGRO
  Belgrade (E)
  Podgorica (C)
  Pristina (BO)
SEYCHELLES
  Victoria (-)
SIERRA LEONE
  Freetown (E)
SINGAPORE
  Singapore (E)
SLOVAK REPUBLIC
  Bratislava (E)
SLOVENIA
  Ljubljana (E)
SOLOMON ISLANDS
  Honiara (-)
SOMALIA
  Mogadishu (-)
SOUTH AFRICA
  Pretoria (E)
  Cape Town (CG)
  Durban (CG)
  Johannesburg (CG)
SPAIN
  Madrid (E)
  Barcelona (CG)
SRI LANKA
  Colombo (E)
SUDAN
  Khartoum (E)
SURINAME
  Paramaribo (E)
SWAZILAND
  Mbabane (E)
SWEDEN
  Stockholm (E)
SWITZERLAND
  Bern (E)
  Geneva (M)
SYRIA
  Damascus (E)
TAIWAN
  Taipei (American
  Institute)
TAJIKISTAN
  Dushanbe (E)
TANZANIA
  Dar es Salaam (E)
THAILAND
  Bangkok (E)
  Chiang Mai (CG)
TOGO
  Lome (E)
TONGA
  Nuku'alofa (-)
TRINIDAD & TOBAGO
  Port-of-Spain (E)
TUNISIA
  Tunis (E)
TURKEY
  Ankara (E)
  Istanbul (CG)
  Adana (C)

TURKMENISTAN
  Ashgabat (E)
TUVALU
  Funafuti (-)
UGANDA
  Kampala (E)
UKRAINE
  Kiev (E)
UNITED ARAB EMIRATES
  Abu Dhabi (E)
  Dubai (CG)
UNITED KINGDOM
  London, England (E)
  Belfast,
  Northern Ireland (CG)
  Edinburgh,
  Scotland (CG)
UNITED STATES OF
AMERICA
  New York (M)
  Washington (M)
URUGUAY
  Montevideo (E)
UZBEKISTAN
  Tashkent (E)
VANUATU
  Port Vila (-)
VENEZUELA
  Caracas (E)
VIETNAM
  Hanoi (E)
  Ho Chi Minh City (CG)
YEMEN
  Sanaa (E)
ZAMBIA
  Lusaka (E)
ZIMBABWE
  Harare (E)

Legend:

Embassy (E)
Consulate General (CG)
Consulate (C)
Mission (M)
Branch Office (BO)
Interest Section (IS)
Liaison Office (LO)
No U.S. Presence (-)

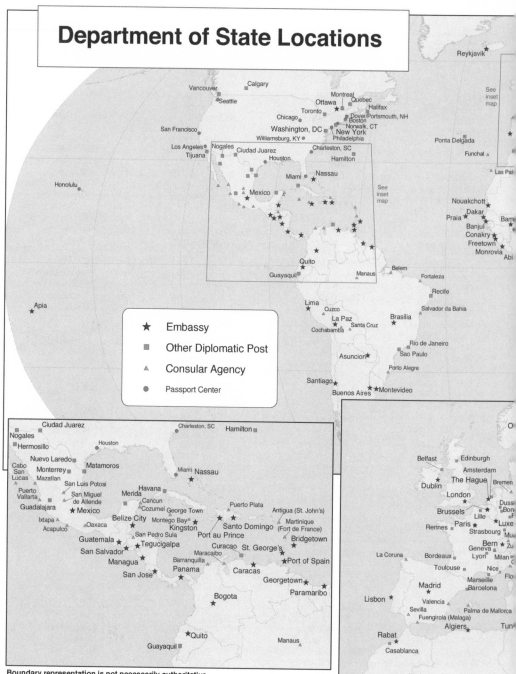

Department of State Locations

★ Embassy

■ Other Diplomatic Post

▲ Consular Agency

● Passport Center

Boundary representation is not necessarily authoritative.

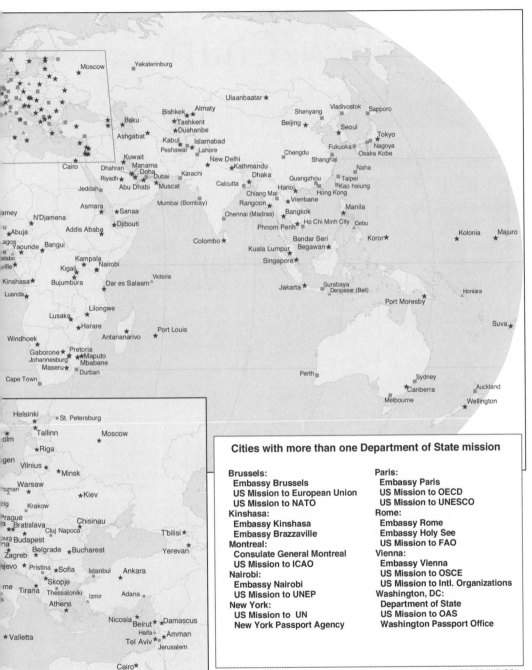

Cities with more than one Department of State mission

Brussels:
 Embassy Brussels
 US Mission to European Union
 US Mission to NATO
Kinshasa:
 Embassy Kinshasa
 Embassy Brazzaville
Montreal:
 Consulate General Montreal
 US Mission to ICAO
Nairobi:
 Embassy Nairobi
 US Mission to UNEP
New York:
 US Mission to UN
 New York Passport Agency

Paris:
 Embassy Paris
 US Mission to OECD
 US Mission to UNESCO
Rome:
 Embassy Rome
 Embassy Holy See
 US Mission to FAO
Vienna:
 Embassy Vienna
 US Mission to OSCE
 US Mission to Intl. Organizations
Washington, DC:
 Department of State
 US Mission to OAS
 Washington Passport Office

6938 2 02 STATE (INR/GGI)

Embassy Flow Chart

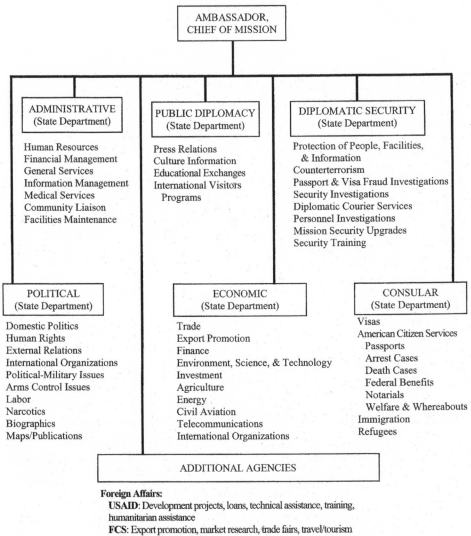

AMBASSADOR,
CHIEF OF MISSION

ADMINISTRATIVE
(State Department)

Human Resources
Financial Management
General Services
Information Management
Medical Services
Community Liaison
Facilities Maintenance

PUBLIC DIPLOMACY
(State Department)

Press Relations
Culture Information
Educational Exchanges
International Visitors
   Programs

DIPLOMATIC SECURITY
(State Department)

Protection of People, Facilities,
   & Information
Counterterrorism
Passport & Visa Fraud Investigations
Security Investigations
Diplomatic Courier Services
Personnel Investigations
Mission Security Upgrades
Security Training

POLITICAL
(State Department)

Domestic Politics
Human Rights
External Relations
International Organizations
Political-Military Issues
Arms Control Issues
Labor
Narcotics
Biographics
Maps/Publications

ECONOMIC
(State Department)

Trade
Export Promotion
Finance
Environment, Science, & Technology
Investment
Agriculture
Energy
Civil Aviation
Telecommunications
International Organizations

CONSULAR
(State Department)

Visas
American Citizen Services
   Passports
   Arrest Cases
   Death Cases
   Federal Benefits
   Notarials
   Welfare & Whereabouts
Immigration
Refugees

ADDITIONAL AGENCIES

Foreign Affairs:
   USAID: Development projects, loans, technical assistance, training,
   humanitarian assistance
   FCS: Export promotion, market research, trade fairs, travel/tourism
   FAS: Food export promotion, agricultural reporting, inspections
   International Broadcasting Bureau: Voice of America
Other:
   DOD: Military Attachés, Marine Security Guards, military sales and assistance,
   medical research
   Homeland Security: Coast Guard, Customs, INS, Secret Service
   **CIA, CDC, DEA, EPA, FAA, FBI, IRS, Library of Congress,
   Peace Corps, Treasury, USTR**

PART 1

Profiles: Who Works in an Embassy?

BY SHAWN DORMAN

T he ambassador is the official and personal envoy of the U.S. president in the country in which he or she serves. It takes a whole team to run an embassy, however, and ambassadors are backed up by professionals handling everything from arranging press briefings to keeping the phones working.

Without a deputy chief of mission, the ambassador could easily become overwhelmed with management tasks. Without an office management specialist as the gatekeeper, the ambassador might end up meeting with the foreign minister's staff assistant when he or she should be meeting with the president of the country. Without the information management staff, the embassy's links to Washington and the rest of the world would come to a screeching halt. Without political officers, the ambassador might not learn about key people needing attention from the U.S. government. Without the consular officers, the lines for visas would stretch on for miles. Without the Foreign Service Nationals (the local staff), the embassy would need to start a knowledge base all over again every few years as American Foreign Service staff rotate out.

Every person working in an embassy plays a vital role, and the following profiles will illustrate just what those roles are. We chose one representative for each key Foreign Service position in an embassy. The people profiled work in embassies and consulates in every region of the world where the U.S. has representation. Some of the largest U.S. embassies have over a thousand employees, while some of the smallest have just a few.

Meet Carmen Martinez, the consul general in Sao Paulo, Brazil, and see that the most interesting happenings do not always take place in the capital city, and consulates can be just as significant to the overall relationship with the country as the embassy in the capital. Meet Lee Boam, running the biggest Foreign Commercial Office in the world in Beijing, where billions of dollars in business contracts are won and lost every day. And meet Labor Officer John Chamberlin, also in Beijing, who tries to help China see that everyone's interest in a stable global trading system will be undermined if workers are not treated fairly. See that it is possible for the U.S. government to promote increased trade with China while at the same time promoting worker rights there. Meet Refugee Coordinator Randy Berry, who spends much of his time assessing conditions in refugee camps and settlements in Central and East Africa. And spend time with Junior Officer DeAngela Burns-Wallace in Embassy Pretoria's public affairs section, as she faces the real-life "tough questions" she was trained to handle.

These are the men and women of the Foreign Service, and these are their jobs.

Ambassador
ANNE W. PATTERSON
EMBASSY BOGOTA, COLOMBIA

The ambassador is the chief of the diplomatic mission and the personal representative of the president of the United States to a foreign country. About 70 percent of ambassadors are career Foreign Service officers, and 30 percent are non-Foreign Service political appointees. As ambassador to Colombia, career FSO Anne Patterson, 52, coordinates U.S. policy, including the operations of other U.S. government agencies in Colombia, and represents the United States to the Colombian government, the business sector, and civil society. At Embassy Bogota, she oversees a staff of close to one thousand, including American and local employees, not counting the several hundred temporary duty personnel who rotate through.

"Colombia is a study in contrasts," says Ambassador Patterson. It is one of the longest-standing democracies in Latin America. Despite what you read in the press, she says, "Colombia is a sophisticated country, rich in art and culture, with a highly developed business and political class." However, more kidnappings occur in Colombia than any other country in the world, and the homicide rate is among the highest in the hemisphere. The weakness of the state and widespread narcotrafficking have spawned and strengthened illegal armed groups. As these groups have grown, they have become a significant military threat to the state. The security of American citizens in Colombia and the embassy staff is always a top priority for the ambassador, who must juggle the sometimes conflicting responsibilities to protect Americans while keeping them accessible. Employees working at Embassy Bogota do so at substantial personal risk. Bogota is one of the few postings that comes with a "danger pay" allowance, the equivalent of U.S. military combat pay.

Colombia is the source of over 80 percent of the cocaine that reaches U.S. shores. The key bilateral issue for the U.S. embassy in Colombia — and for the ambassador — is reducing the flow of narcotics to the United States from Colombia. "In 2000, the U.S. government began to invest major resources in fighting drugs and contributing to broad reforms of Colombian society," Anne comments. Colombia now ranks number three for U.S. assistance, with the U.S. foreign aid investment approaching $2 billion. The core element of U.S. assistance, Plan Colombia, is a drug eradication program that also has components to help modernize the police, the military and the judiciary. The ambassador must supervise the implementation of the program, ensuring that it runs smoothly and meets U.S. government objectives. She therefore puts a premium on interagency cooperation, especially given Plan Colombia's wide scope. "This is an ambitious program which has the potential to help the Colombians improve their difficult situation," she says.

"American ambassadors and the people who work for them have prevented coups, saved lives, and very substantially transformed some of the countries in which they have served."

Embassy Bogotá is a large embassy with 22 U.S. government agencies represented, including most American law enforcement agencies. The post has grown rapidly over the past two years: There are currently over 200 people at post working on the drug eradication program, including about 100 from the Drug Enforcement Administration. The ambassador must always know what each agency at post is doing and be prepared to respond to inquiries — many coming from Congress — on the status and progress of programs.

"An American ambassador is a combination chief executive and cheerleader for American interests," says Anne. "There have been many cases in which American ambassadors and the people who work for them have prevented coups, saved lives, and very substantially transformed some of the countries in which they have served," she adds.

The U.S. ambassador in Colombia, as in other countries, is a public figure. "I spend considerable time articulating U.S. policy to business groups and the press," says Anne. "This is particularly true when American policy is controversial, as it is in Colombia." She meets with Colombian government officials regularly, and just about every day attends at least one event sponsored by the government, the business community or others in the embassy.

Ambassador Patterson acts as host to many congressional and other official visitors from the U.S. She often briefs visitors on the current situation on the ground, and brings in the appropriate embassy staff members to participate in such briefings.

"In an embassy of this size, there is no substitute for face-to-face communications," says Anne, who makes time in her extremely full schedule to meet daily with senior embassy staff. The ambassador tries to encourage her staff to be involved in the conceptualization of the next steps for U.S. policy and she fosters an atmosphere in which both dissenting and new ideas can flourish. "The best ideas very often come from the Americans working in the embassy," she notes. Sometimes alternative concepts make their way into policy.

Ambassador Patterson has been in the Foreign Service since 1973, and she has "loved every minute of it." Before she became ambassador to Colombia in 2000, she served as U.S. ambassador to El Salvador. She has served as the principal deputy assistant secretary for the Bureau of Western Hemisphere Affairs and as director of the Office of Andean Affairs. She has also served in the U.S. mission to the United Nations in Geneva, Switzerland, and in Riyadh, Saudi Arabia. Her first assignment was as an economic officer in Quito, Ecuador. She was born in Fort Smith, Arkansas, and is married to retired Foreign Service officer David R. Patterson, who is also from Fort Smith. They have two sons, ages 15 and 20.

Deputy Chief of Mission
DANIEL R. RUSSEL
EMBASSY NICOSIA, CYPRUS

The deputy chief of mission (DCM) at an embassy is second in command and serves as the chief operating officer of the embassy, coordinating the different embassy sections and varying goals in an effort to create one strong united team. The DCM must always know what's going on inside and outside the embassy, keeping the "big picture" in mind. "Without a DCM, the ambassador risks becoming overwhelmed with management tasks, and section heads would be left to their own devices to pursue priorities and make decisions that may not reflect the larger policy or management interests of the U.S. government," explains Danny Russel, the DCM at Embassy Nicosia.

Danny Russel, 48, works closely with the ambassador, serving as his "alter ego," frequently substituting for him — serving as acting ambassador, or chargé d'affaires, when the ambassador is absent from the country — and speaking for him in setting out requirements and priorities. The DCM also has "a responsibility to offer creative dissent when appropriate and make sure the ambassador has considered counter-arguments and potential risks before making a decision," Danny notes. "Once a decision is made, it is my job to ensure it is carried out effectively."

The ambassador relies on the DCM to keep him informed and to be the key liaison with all sections of the embassy. In practical terms, Danny's role — and that of most DCMs — is to get the maximum performance from all elements of the mission by keeping them all coordinated; ensuring that Washington gets the information, advice and support it needs; providing feedback and reality checks to the ambassador; intervening when needed to head off or resolve problems; serving as crisis manager; and attending to the security, morale and well-being of the embassy community. "If you can't find 10 minutes for any of your people, you shouldn't be a DCM," he maintains. In his more public role, Danny is constantly engaged with the host government, the media, various local groups, American citizens and business representatives, and diplomats from other countries.

Embassy Nicosia is a medium-size embassy housed in a heavily fortified but attractive building on a compound close to downtown. Cyprus is a small, divided Mediterranean island. The "Cyprus Problem" — the standoff between the Greek-Cypriot and Turkish-Cypriot sides of Cyprus — is the key substantive issue facing the embassy. The island is split into two heavily armed camps, one backed by Greece and the other by Turkey, and separated by a buffer zone patrolled by U.N. peacekeepers. The embassy is active working with both sides and the U.N. negotiators to help promote a peaceful settlement and to reduce tensions and the risk of a military incident. "We must operate as a dual embassy in many respects," Danny explains, "because there are two distinct languages and cultures on the island."

The embassy also handles a range of transnational challenges confronting embassies

worldwide, such as terrorism, narcotics, arms shipments, environmental destruction, and illegal immigration. The DCM must coordinate the U.S. response to all of these issues.

Danny chairs the embassy's Emergency Action Committee and the Law Enforcement Working Group, and is responsible for managing embassy security. He is also the primary point of contact at the embassy for the State Department's Bureau of European Affairs. Every morning he receives an "overnight note" from the Cyprus Desk in Washington, which provides feedback, guidance, questions and "action requests" (sometimes called taskings). The DCM distributes these to the appropriate section or individual, who must ensure the appropriate action is taken, whether it is a political officer making a demarche to the host government, an administrative officer arranging vehicles for an official visitor, or any number of highly varied requirements. At the end of the day, he sends a short report back to the desk responding to questions, flagging new issues, and conveying an informal heads-up on items of interest. Most evenings, he attends at least one event: a diplomatic reception, a drop-by at someone's party, a dinner or concert, or a Marine House TGIF party.

The DCM has a highly demanding job, and must be able to juggle numerous issues at once. "The Foreign Service is very rich in talent, and one of the great joys of being the DCM is being able to harness the energy, talent, and know-how of the team," says Danny. While it's a serious job, "you also need to have a sense of humor, so that you don't take yourself too seriously and so you can put people at ease and help them work together without friction."

After college, Danny was seized with wanderlust and set out to travel the world, getting as far as Japan, where he studied martial arts and Japanese. He spent six years working for

Checking in with the Marine at Post One.

a Japanese firm in New York City, and "gradually came to worry that the Japanese were doing too good a job figuring out America while we Americans were not doing enough to learn about the world and protect our interests." This led him to the Foreign Service. Since joining in 1985, he has served in Tokyo and Osaka, Japan; the U.S. Mission to the United Nations in New York; Seoul, South Korea; and Washington, D.C. He was chief of staff to Under Secretary of State for Political Affairs Tom Pickering, and spent a year as a Cox Fellow, writing the book *America's Place in the World*, published by Georgetown University. He attended Sarah Lawrence College and the University of London. He and his wife, Keiko, have three children. His next posting is as DCM for Embassy The Hague, Netherlands.

Consul General
CARMEN MARIA MARTINEZ
CONSULATE GENERAL SAO PAULO, BRAZIL

Carmen Martinez will tell you she's got one of the best jobs around. "There's a lot of autonomy, a wide variety of issues to deal with, and the consul general sets the tone." Most people know that ambassadors run U.S. embassies, but not so many understand the key role of the consuls general, also known as principal officers, who manage U.S. consulates, the U.S. offices located outside of capital cities in countries around the world.

Carmen Martinez runs U.S. Consulate General Sao Paulo, one of the largest U.S. consulates in the world. She has returned to the post of her first Foreign Service assignment 22 years ago. The consulate is staffed by 70 Americans and over 180 Foreign Service Nationals. Sao Paulo is the fourth largest city in the world and the commercial and cultural center of Brazil. The embassy and the Foreign Ministry may be in the capital, Brasilia, but it's clear that much of the action is in the cosmopolitan, sophisticated, bustling, traffic-jammed, crime-ridden city of Sao Paulo. The city is home to extreme wealth as well as extreme poverty. Crime and security are among the biggest problems affecting both official and unofficial Americans in the consular district, and Carmen estimates she spends as much as 30 percent of her time dealing with those issues.

The consul general "runs the show" at a consulate, but always supports the ambassador's policy and operational objectives by coordinating closely with the embassy. Carmen describes a key part of her job as showing the face of America in an accurate and sympathetic way. She is a strong advocate of public diplomacy efforts such as speaking engagements, television appearances, videoconferences, and other media outreach. "I keep on telling the staff to seek out opportunities for public outreach — get out there and be an active and visible representative of the United States." And her other message is to have fun. "A lot of laughter helps," she says. "Be willing to let your personality and values show in your leadership style."

For the principal officer in a huge cosmopolitan center like Sao Paulo, the representational responsibilities are heavy because the city draws so many official visitors, especially those interested in trade and culture. Carmen hosts an event at least once or twice a week in honor of trade missions in town seeking business opportunities, congressional visitors, or cultural happenings. She sees representational events as critical morale builders, and tries to include as many different members of the consulate community as she can, including local employees, junior officers, and family members.

During a typical day, Carmen will check in with the embassy in Brasilia; talk with consular officers or visit the consular section (Sao Paulo has one of the busiest non-immigrant visa sections in the world, and the American citizens services unit has 17,000 Americans registered in the consular district); read and clear outgoing cables/reports; sign numerous official papers; make personnel and budget decisions; meet with American Chamber of Commerce representatives; give a speech at a seminar; and host or attend a representational function.

Carmen is especially proud of the excellent interagency cooperation between State and Commerce (which has its third largest commercial office in the world in Sao Paulo) as well as between State and the numerous other agencies present at the mission, including the Department of Agriculture, the Drug Enforcement Administration, the Customs Service, and the Defense Department. "We have great people here who never forget we are all working for the same government."

Her enthusiasm for her job and for the Foreign Service is contagious, and an obvious motivator for her staff. "I've been in the Foreign Service almost 22 years and I'm still having a good time," Carmen says. She sees mentoring junior officers as a rewarding part of her job and is always glad to discuss future assignments with JOs, guide them through the bidding process, and stay in touch with them even after they leave post. "I take pride in their success and it feels good to think I played a part in it," she says.

Making opening remarks at the 2001 international seminar "Gender in the World Labour Market."

The principal officer is the highest-ranking U.S. official in the host city, so she must always be working to implement and advance U.S. policy. However, being a good manager is an equally important part of being a good principal officer. "If people feel valued, they will do a good job," Carmen believes. "Give your people the tools to do their job, whether it's the person who delivers the mail or the one who delivers the political demarche. Everyone is important."

Carmen joined the Foreign Service in 1980. Her first post was Sao Paulo. She has served as deputy chief of mission in Maputo, Mozambique; and as consul general at the U.S. consulate in Barranquilla, Colombia, before it was closed for security reasons. She has also served in Quito, Ecuador; Bangkok, Thailand; Caracas, Venezuela, and Washington, D.C. Carmen has a B.A. in liberal arts, an M.A. in medieval history, and an M.S. in national security and strategic resources. She speaks Portuguese, Spanish and Thai. She and her husband, Victor Reimer, have one son. Her next assignment is as chargé d'affaires to Burma.

U.S. Agency for International Development Mission Director

Desaix "Terry" Myers

Embassy Jakarta, Indonesia

The U.S. Agency for International Development (USAID) is the federal government agency that provides economic, development, and humanitarian assistance around the world in support of the foreign policy goals of the United States. The agency's headquarters are in Washington, D.C., but the heart of the work is done through the USAID field offices around the world. USAID has its own distinct Foreign Service, and USAID employees work in partnership with private voluntary organizations, indigenous organizations, universities, American businesses, international agencies, other governments, and other U.S. government agencies. The main office of USAID in any country, known as the "mission,"

On a site visit to USAID-funded flood relief efforts.

is part of the U.S. embassy and is run by a mission director, or a representative in the case of smaller programs.

USAID missions are responsible for developing strategies, managing program implementation, and evaluating results of U.S. government-funded assistance programs, in conjunction with local counterparts. Program areas include providing humanitarian assistance, promoting democracy and good governance, encouraging economic growth, protecting the environment, and improving health conditions.

In Indonesia, the agency was in the process of phasing out its highly successful long-term assistance program in the late 1990s when the Asian financial crisis and the fall of President Suharto changed the Indonesian context dramatically. These days, USAID is needed more than ever in Indonesia, but programming has changed and priorities have shifted based on the situation on the ground.

The USAID mission in Jakarta is run by Mission Director Terry Myers, 56, who oversees programs for Indonesia as well as East Timor, which became independent in 2001. USAID is helping East Timor rebuild a shattered economy and infrastructure, create jobs, and develop a constitution and democratic institutions. The Indonesia USAID mission, housed in a building on the embassy compound, is fairly large, staffed by 21 Foreign Service officers, 30 contractors working inside the mission, and 120 Indonesians.

The main tasks of the mission director, according to Terry, are to "listen, coordinate, inform and adjudicate." He works closely with international donors, Indonesian government officials, non-governmental organizations, Indonesian and international companies, and the media to assess where USAID assistance is most appropriate and needed. He coordinates USAID's activities with those of other donors and with the Indonesian government.

The USAID Indonesia program is broad and complex. Indonesia is attempting a threefold transition: to democracy, following 33 years of autocracy under President Suharto;

USAID helped
Indonesia successfully
carry out its first free
and fair elections
in 1999.

to a decentralized government, following decades of command and control from Jakarta; and to a free and open economy, following one of the worst economic collapses in the last century. USAID helped Indonesia successfully carry out its first free and fair elections in 1999 by supporting local non-governmental organizations as well as U.S.-based organizations experienced in creating democratic election systems. USAID provides technical advisors to the Indonesian government and to civil society organizations engaged in a wide array of issues key to the creation of democratic institutions: financial sector reform; legal and judicial reform; political party development; and development of free and responsible media. In addition, USAID programs focus on environmental protection and health and humanitarian assistance.

Terry regularly attends meetings with government officials and non-governmental organization representatives working on USAID-supported projects. He also has a visible public role, opening seminars, cutting ribbons, and talking to the media about USAID activities. He briefs numerous official visitors from Congress, USAID, the State Department, and other government agencies, and must interpret and integrate their concerns into the country program.

"The job provides a constant stream of intriguing problems to be resolved — strategic, tactical, logistical, personnel, budget, substantive as well as trivial," Terry says. He must constantly sort out the most critical problems, dealing with immediate concerns while trying to keep perspective on the long-term objectives. Terry handles vastly varied subjects every day, from issues involving assistance to refugees in far-flung islands beset with conflict to problems of widespread corruption, illegal logging, trafficking in persons, legal reform, maternal and child health, educational reform and development of democratic institutions, and more mundane but often contentious questions of who gets what residence, and whether USAID is contributing enough to the embassy's administrative budget.

Terry joined USAID in 1969 and has served overseas in Dakar, Senegal; Dhaka, East Pakistan (before it was Bangladesh); and New Delhi, India, where he was deputy mission director for four years. This is his second tour in Jakarta. In Washington, he worked on USAID's first Russia program in the early 1990s. He took ten years off from USAID during the 1970s to help start a private, nonprofit research company, which reports to institutional investors on issues of corporate social responsibility. He also worked as an adjunct professor at Georgetown University. He has published three books and numerous articles. Terry has a B.A. from the University of California at Berkeley and a Ph.D. from the Fletcher School of Law and Diplomacy at Tufts University. He and his wife, Lynn, have three children. His next posting will be as USAID Mission Director to Moscow.

Political Officer

EARLE C. "CHAT" BLAKEMAN
EMBASSY ISLAMABAD, PAKISTAN

The job of the political officer is to provide the U.S. government with current analysis of the host country's domestic and foreign policies, to identify opportunities to advance U.S. interests, and to actively promote those interests in the host country. Political officers are the resident experts on the host country's recent history and political developments. They have diverse roles, as reporting officers and action officers, combining the skills of journalists, analysts, and public relations specialists. Political officers tell the story — letting Washington know what's happening on the ground and what it needs to know to make policy — but also present and advocate U.S. policy to host country representatives.

Chat (left) meets with security officials at the Islamabad airport moments before Secretary of State Colin Powell arrives.

It has been a highly charged, dangerous, and challenging year for everyone at Embassy Islamabad, a medium-size embassy that sits on a 34-acre compound right against the Himalayan foothills. Three issues currently dominate the U.S. agenda: fighting the war against terrorism, seeking to prevent an open conflict — including the possibility of nuclear war — between Pakistan and India, and supporting the transition to democratic civilian rule in Pakistan.

Relations between the U.S. and Pakistan were strained for many years, and Embassy Islamabad's political officers have worked hard to help move the relationship in a new, more productive direction. The U.S.-Pakistan relationship serves as a particularly good example of the tension that can exist between serving specific political objectives, like fighting terrorism, and remaining consistent regarding U.S. positions on democracy and human rights. Political officers must work for the political objective without letting go of broader goals of promoting democracy and human rights — not always an easy balance to strike.

Political Counselor Chat Blakeman, 50, head of Embassy Islamabad's political section, explains that the primary role for political officers in Islamabad in the war against terrorism has been to work with FBI, military, and others to identify ways the U.S. and Pakistan could cooperate in efforts to track down al-Qaida and other terrorists who fled Afghanistan for Pakistan when the Taliban collapsed. Prior to the re-opening of Embassy Kabul in early 2002, political officers in Pakistan had responsibility for tracking events inside Afghanistan and supporting efforts to bring about a stable government there.

The U.S. often plays the role of mediator in conflicts around the world, and political officers facilitate the process. Embassy Islamabad political officers have worked with colleagues in New Delhi and Washington to find ways to help India and Pakistan step back from the brink of war. "Secretary Colin Powell, Deputy Secretary Richard Armitage, and Assistant Secretary for South Asian Affairs Christina Rocca have devoted countless hours to helping resolve this issue, and we have tried to support them," says Chat. Political officers facilitate

The U.S. often plays the role of mediator in conflicts around the world, and political officers facilitate the process.

high-level meetings by keeping the U.S. government informed about developments, identifying areas for possible cooperation, and overseeing the visits. They do everything from setting up appointments and briefing VIP visitors on the situation to taking notes during meetings and writing the reports on them, and conducting follow-up meetings.

Political officers also play public roles, presenting U.S. positions to sometimes-skeptical audiences. "During the height of Operation Enduring Freedom in Afghanistan," Chat says, "our political officers regularly spoke at local universities, for example, to explain what the U.S. was doing and to answer questions. These audiences were sometimes quite hostile, but that is precisely why we were there."

Since September 11, security issues have dominated life at Embassy Islamabad. During the past 12 months, family members and all non-emergency staff have been evacuated twice. The second evacuation followed a church bombing in March 2002 two blocks from the embassy, which killed two beloved members of the embassy community. The political section is functioning at about half-strength because of the evacuation. Due to the seemingly endless crisis environment and the pared-down staff, political officers in Islamabad work six or seven days a week most of the time.

Chat visits the Pakistan Ministry of Foreign Affairs most days to discuss pending issues, ranging from an upcoming VIP visit to a request for Pakistan to support the U.S. position on a United Nations vote. He often meets with political party leaders to gain insight into current thinking. "Policy-makers and analysts in Washington want to know who is likely to win the election and what the results will mean for Pakistan and our interests here. We do our best to tell them," Chat says.

Human rights are a special concern in the U.S. relationship with Pakistan, particularly the treatment of women. Political officers meet with victims of abuses and their families, track dozens of cases, and report the stories. "Our real goal is to improve the situation," says Chat. "We are doing that through a number of programs that strengthen democratic institutions and raise the profile of human rights. Our biggest successes have come in working with Pakistan to reduce trafficking in persons and child labor."

Chat has a B.A. in English literature and an M.A. in international relations from the University of Pennsylvania. He worked as a journalist and business consultant prior to joining the Foreign Service in 1985. He has served overseas in Bogota, Colombia; New Delhi, India; and Port Louis, Mauritius. He has served in Washington at the State Department and the National Security Council. He and his wife, Laura, have a 12-year-old daughter.

Economic Officer

MARY WARLICK

EMBASSY MOSCOW, RUSSIA

Embassy Moscow is one of the largest and busiest embassies in the world. The bilateral economic agenda with Russia is one of the highest priorities in the U.S.-Russia relationship. Economic officers at Embassy Moscow, explains Economic Minister-Counselor Mary Warlick, report on the country's economic reform efforts, which are an important indicator of Russia's transformation to a sustainable democracy and market economy. Economic officers in Moscow are also actively engaged in advancing U.S. trade and investment objectives in Russia, in coordination with the Foreign Commercial Service, the Foreign Agricultural Service, and the American business community in Russia.

Mary, 45, manages Embassy Moscow's 22-person economic section, which includes a reform unit, a trade and investment unit, a Treasury Department attaché and the embassy's coordinator for U.S. assistance programs in Russia.

Most American ambassadors are charged with working to expand the trade and investment opportunities for U.S. companies in their country of assignment. Nowhere is this more true than in Russia. As a result, Mary and her economic team spend much of their time advocating to the Russian government policy changes that will improve the investment climate for U.S. businesses.

Sensitive to the fact that one cannot know Russia by staying in Moscow, Mary travels regularly to different regions of the country, and encourages her staff to do the same. In addition to their own meetings with Russian government officials, economists and business people, Mary and her staff often accompany the ambassador to his meetings with senior officials or business leaders, which present unique opportunities to advance U.S. economic policy objectives.

Mary has responsibility for the embassy's reporting and analysis of the pace and progress of the Russian government's economic program — including banking, land, pension, and tax reforms. She and her staff also play a key role in efforts to resolve outstanding trade and investment disputes between U.S. and Russian companies; assist Russia in its WTO accession process; protect U.S. intellectual property rights; manage ongoing trade disputes on issues such as poultry and steel; advance energy cooperation and improve the climate for foreign investment in the Russian energy sector; and support the private sector Russian-American Business and Banking dialogues.

Each of these issues draws high-level interest from Washington, which leads to a steady stream of official visitors to Moscow. Many of these visits are supported by the embassy's economic staff, who help determine which Russian officials each delegation should meet and provide briefing materials and oral briefings on the current situation to the visitors. During the past year, the economic section supported numerous visits by senior U.S. government policy-makers, including the U.S. trade representative; the secretary of commerce; the secretary

"Every assignment has brought new challenges and opportunities that have exposed me to new issues and parts of the world."

of energy; as well as sub-Cabinet level officials from the State Department, Treasury, Commerce, the U.S. Export-Import Bank, the Overseas Private Investment Corporation, and the Trade and Development Agency.

One key accomplishment in 2002 was convincing Russia to lift a ban on U.S. poultry imports (worth over $600 million in 2001) that it had imposed without warning in early March. The dispute received top-level attention, including the personal engagement of Secretary Colin Powell. As with many issues in the economic relationship, this one required close coordination and cooperation among U.S. government agencies, in this case State, the Departments of Agriculture and Commerce, and the U.S. Trade Representative's office.

Mary's days are busy and often quite long. She usually begins the day reviewing e-mail, cable traffic, and press reports to identify action requests or other issues requiring the attention of the economic section. She checks in with her staff to discuss the day's priorities, and then begins what is usually a full schedule of meetings. She holds a weekly staff meeting with the economic section and participates in the ambassador's "country team meeting" of senior staff, held twice a week. Between meetings, she finds time to review reports and briefing memos written by her staff. Several times a week she provides briefings on the economic situation in Russia to visiting U.S. government officials or American business representatives. At about 4 or 5 p.m. in Moscow, she connects with colleagues at the State Department's Russia Desk or at the National Security Council to review developments and identify time-sensitive issues requiring the embassy's attention. Following a long work day, Mary and her husband, James, the consul general in Moscow, frequently attend evening representational events at the ambassador's residence or elsewhere in Moscow.

"I find it hard to imagine a more exciting and interesting career path," Mary says. "Every

assignment has brought new challenges and opportunities that have exposed me to new issues and parts of the world, while at the same time helping me become a better manager of people and foreign policy issues."

Mary joined the Foreign Service in 1983. She has served in Manila, Philippines (twice); Dhaka, Bangladesh; Bonn, Germany; and Washington, D.C. Her hometown is Eau Claire, Wisconsin, but she was born and raised in Papua New Guinea as the daughter of Lutheran missionaries. She has a B.A. in political science from Valparaiso University in Indiana and an M.A. from the Fletcher School of Law and Diplomacy, where she met her husband. They have three children, ages 9, 14, and 15.

Mary in front of the Russian parliament building.

Commercial Officer
THOMAS L. "LEE" BOAM
EMBASSY BEIJING, CHINA

The U.S.-China relationship is one of the most critical and complex in the world. Numerous groups — from members of Congress and human rights and non-governmental organizations to political appointees in the administration — have strong and sometimes contentious views on issues impacting the U.S.-China relationship. The commercial connection with China is often the adhesive that sees the relationship through difficult periods, says Embassy Beijing's senior commercial officer, Lee Boam.

The job of the senior commercial officer in China is highly visible, and Lee, 55, must often deliver highly political messages through commercial channels. China's economy is booming and countless U.S. firms are seeking opportunities there. U.S. business representatives often come to China excited about the potential market of 1.3 billion people, but without a basic understanding of the realities of working there. Issues of language, distance from the U.S., cultural differences, lack of transparency, and the peculiarities of local provincial markets make doing business in China one of the most unique and difficult, but potentially rewarding, challenges for U.S. business in the world.

Lee and Foreign Service National Bai Ying at a U.S.-China housing initiative.

A key part of the commercial officer's job in China and elsewhere is to help shepherd U.S. companies — the "clients" of the Foreign Commercial Service — through the maze of difficulties faced when trying to do business in the host country, and to help these companies strengthen their market position. Each company has different goals, and the commercial officer tailors assistance to the individual needs of each company. Commercial assistance in China ranges from conducting market research and identifying potential partners to advocating on a company's behalf with a government ministry or introducing company representatives to the right Chinese government officials.

Aside from helping U.S. companies, the commercial officer in China must work to further U.S. trade policies and ensure compliance with existing trade commitments; monitor World Trade Organization compliance; identify and report on industry trends; and conduct negotiations on such issues as intellectual property protection, antidumping, and export controls. The Foreign Commercial Service also represents the Export-Import Bank as well as the Trade Development Agency, two independent government agencies that offer financing and trade assistance to U.S. companies.

The Department of Commerce has been the home base for commercial officers since 1980, when they were moved from the State Department. The work did not change, and commercial officers still make up a small but key element of the Foreign Service team at embassies around the world. Due to the importance of the economic and trade

> At any given time, Lee is advocating on behalf of American companies bidding on major projects worth billions of dollars, and also has several billion dollars' worth of trade disputes on his desk.

relationship with China, Embassy Beijing is home to the largest Foreign Commercial Service office in the world. About 100 people, including Americans and Foreign Service Nationals, work for the Foreign Commercial Service in Beijing and in the consulates in Guangzhou, Shanghai, Shenyang, and Chengdu. The Foreign Commercial Service accounts for almost 20 percent of the total staff of the embassy and the consulates in China. As the senior commercial officer in the country, Lee has oversight over the entire Foreign Commercial Service operation, at the embassy and at all the consulates.

At any given time, Lee is advocating on behalf of American companies bidding on major projects worth billions of dollars, and also has several billion dollars' worth of trade disputes on his desk. More trade disputes are brought to the Commercial Service in China than anywhere else in the world. "This is the dilemma of China," he says, "huge successes and huge failures. The potential for tremendous contracts — like the $1.3 billion contract for the sale of Boeing aircraft or the $1 billion contract to outfit the Shenzhen subway system — keeps businesses coming." U.S. business reps often tell Beijing's commercial office staff that successful sales and contracts would not have been possible without their help.

Lee has initiated an extensive program to brief American business representatives before they set out for China. Over the past year, Lee (during trips to the U.S.) and his colleagues have talked to over 3,000 participants at various seminars in the U.S., providing guidance to companies on business opportunities and on avoiding pitfalls.

Before joining the Foreign Commercial Service in 1982, Lee worked for a large American company that provided archival microfilming to governments, where he was responsible for international operations. In this capacity, he spent time in 87 countries. He joined the Foreign Commercial Service because he saw it as an opportunity not to just help one company succeed, but to help many companies, in all industry sectors. Lee served in Stuttgart and Frankfurt, Germany, and was later sent back to Germany as con-

Lee with the Embassy Beijing FCS staff.

sul general to reopen the consulate in Dusseldorf. He was the first and last commercial officer assigned to then-East Germany, just prior to reunification, and has also served in Hong Kong.

Lee was born in Fort Collins, Colorado, but calls Wyoming home. He has a B.A. and M.B.A. from the University of Utah and a Ph.D. in organizational leadership from the University of Oklahoma. He and his wife, Myrna, have four children.

Agricultural Officer
HOLLY HIGGINS
EMBASSY SOFIA, BULGARIA

The Foreign Agricultural Service (FAS) has just over 100 Foreign Service officers serving at embassies in almost 50 countries. FAS Foreign Service officers represent the U.S. Department of Agriculture overseas and handle all agricultural policy and trade issues in their assigned regions. "We help support U.S. agricultural trade and contribute to food security around the world through food aid programs," says Regional Agricultural Attaché Holly Higgins of Embassy Sofia. Overseas, the Foreign Agricultural Service represents the entire U.S. farm sector: farmers, food processors, and agricultural exporters. FAS officers work to improve foreign market access for U.S. products, build new markets, and improve the competitive position of U.S. agriculture in the global marketplace. They collect and analyze market information and statistics on agriculture in their region. The FAS mission also includes building food security throughout the world.

Like most FAS offices today, the Embassy Sofia office has regional responsibilities, covering agricultural affairs in Serbia, Montenegro, Kosovo, Albania, Moldova, Macedonia, Romania, and Bulgaria. Holly, 42, is based in Sofia with one other regional FAS officer. She oversees the work of seven Foreign Service National employees, two in Sofia and five in other FAS offices in the region. The FAS office relies heavily on the local staff, explains Holly, noting that "the FSNs in this part of the world are outstanding."

Holly and her staff prepare reports on agricultural trade in the region and monitor the status of crops. Their reporting covers policy changes in the region, marketing opportunities for U.S. agricultural exports, and any other developments that might have an impact on U.S. agricultural trade. The FAS representatives in the field serve as a critical link between foreign buyers and potential suppliers in the U.S. They must always be ready to respond quickly to requests for information from agricultural policy-makers back home.

The FAS Sofia staff travel frequently. Holly is on the road more than 50 percent of the time, visiting Black Sea ports, large farms, and slaughterhouses, and meeting regularly with key government contacts throughout her region. In summertime, she and her staff travel to wheat-and-corn-producing areas along the Danube River to review their estimates for the upcoming harvests, estimates that policy-makers in Washington use to monitor worldwide crop developments and their possible impact on world and U.S. prices.

Holly calls herself a "virtual" attaché, given the wide area she covers and the amount of time she's traveling from country to country. Every day she communicates by e-mail, fax or cell phone with contacts in the embassies in the region and with host government officials. "We joke and say that on a good day, only three U.S. ambassadors are mad at us because we are not in 'their' country," says Holly. As budgets have fallen and posts have closed, regional responsibilities for FAS offices have increased, complicating the balancing act necessary to be a full-time agricultural "consultant" to several ambassadors, often thousands of miles apart.

Holly is on the road more than 50 percent of the time, visiting Black Sea ports, large farms, and slaughterhouses, and meeting with government contacts.

Most of the U.S. agricultural trade in Holly's region is in meat and poultry. Therefore, animal health and food safety issues are paramount for the Sofia office. Holly works closely with the national veterinary agencies in the different countries she covers. One of her office's key achievements has been helping to keep the market open for U.S. meat and poultry by negotiating a bilateral agreement on veterinary certification with the government of Bulgaria.

Administering food aid programs is another important part of Holly's job. The U.S. is the world's largest food aid donor, and in 2002, FAS Sofia supervised over $30 million in food aid. FAS supports direct feeding programs and school lunch programs in Albania, Romania, Bulgaria, and Moldova, which aim to assist vulnerable populations.

Another key agricultural issue for the U.S. in Bulgaria is that of tariff and non-tariff barriers facing U.S. poultry exports. The Bulgarian government maintains a high tariff on U.S. poultry products, which the U.S. industry wants reduced. Holly negotiates, monitors, and reports on this issue. Another key issue for FAS in the region is the increasing influence of European Union regulations in the formation of regional meat and livestock regulations that are not consistent with World Trade Organization rules and discriminate against U.S. products.

Agricultural officers often represent other U.S. Department of Agriculture agencies, such as the Forest Service and the Food Safety Inspection Service. They also coordinate and direct USDA's responsibilities in international trade negotiations, working closely with the U.S. Trade Representative's office. "The FAS officer has to be a jack of all trades in the field of agriculture," explains Holly. They must always be prepared to respond to any agricultural issue of interest to the U.S. that arises in their region. "Issues such as biotechnology and genetic engineering require that we constantly upgrade our understanding of the science and the global regulatory issues," she added.

Holly meets with agribusinessmen in Kosovo.

Individuals must work for the USDA for 18 months before they can apply for the FAS Foreign Service. Holly joined the Foreign Agricultural Service in 1983. Before joining USDA, she was an economist with the Commodity Futures Trading Commission in Chicago. Previous Foreign Service postings include Milan, Italy, and Paris, France. Holly is from Iowa and grew up on a farm. She has a B.A. in economics from the University of Iowa. She is married to Alan Chadwick. They have three young children.

Consular Officer
DON JACOBSON
CONSULATE GENERAL GUADALAJARA, MEXICO

Consulate General Guadalajara serves one of the largest U.S. expatriate communities in the world, with a population of approximately 50,000 resident Americans and a similar number of tourists in the area at any given time. It is responsible for four states in western central Mexico. As consular section chief, Don Jacobson manages over 50 employees. He is responsible for ensuring that both the American citizen services unit in Guadalajara and the consular agency in Puerto Vallarta provide the best possible service to American citizens, whether they are renewing their passports or trying to repatriate the remains of a loved one who passed away while visiting Mexico. He also oversees the non-immigrant visa and fraud prevention units of the consular section, which play an important role in keeping America's borders safe. Guadalajara's non-immigrant visa unit processed over 227,000 applications in Fiscal Year 2001, making it one of the top 10 posts in the world for visa application volume.

In front of the visa windows at Consulate General Guadalajara.

The number-one job for all consular officers worldwide is to protect American citizens and their interests. Consular officers provide a wide range of emergency services to Americans, accept passport applications, and register the births of Americans born overseas. Consular officers also provide visa services to host country residents. They process visa applications for tourists, students, business travelers and other temporary visitors, as well as immigrant visa applications for those who qualify for legal permanent resident status. In deciding who qualifies for a visa, consular officers play a critical role in protecting America's borders.

"Our highest priority in the visa section is to keep out the 'bad guys,'" says Don. "We work closely with the Drug Enforcement Administration and other U.S. law enforcement agencies." The next highest priority is to facilitate legitimate travel. "Given the importance of our economic relationship with Mexico, it is crucial to both our countries that legitimate travelers be able to cross the border with a minimum of hassle. As a result, we have put a lot of effort into making the visa process more transparent and efficient."

The consular section is the public face of any embassy or consulate. The majority of interactions between the post and the local community happen in the consular section, so the quality of service provided by the consular section to visa applicants has a significant impact on how local residents perceive the U.S. Thousands of people around the world line up every day at U.S. embassies and consulates for visa interviews, and consular officers must be ready to conduct the interviews every day. For many visa applicants around the world, the visa interview is their first interaction with an

American and will leave a lasting impression. "We can't afford not to treat them with courtesy and dignity, regardless of the outcome of the interview," Don says.

At a busy consular section like Guadalajara, a visa officer will usually do more than a hundred interviews a day. The work is challenging and can be stressful. The officers know that every interview matters, that they are the first line of defense against the wrong people getting permission to enter the U.S. Many seasoned officers cite the experience gained "on the line" as having a crucial impact on their long-term abilities to make judgments, think on their feet, and speak a foreign language. Still, innovative consular managers like Don are getting junior officers involved in post reporting and in managing the section, so that they are not spending all their time on the visa line.

Consular officers have significant management responsibilities, including management of employees and resources. The consular section is usually the only revenue-generating section of an embassy or consulate. The fees collected for visa processing and other services are used by the State Department to help consular sections improve their operating systems, including security and computer upgrades. Don joined the Foreign Service thinking he was most suited for economic work, but chose the consular career path because he sees it as offering the greatest opportunities to practice innovative management, to motivate his staff, and to improve the efficiency of operations.

At ConGen Guadalajara, Don works to improve customer service and teamwork throughout the consulate, and takes pride in the strong team environment. Mentoring junior officers is an important part of the job of consular managers. Don believes the leadership and management practices that junior officers encounter early in their careers (and most junior officers spend an early tour in a consular section) have a big impact on the kind of leaders and managers they become later in their careers.

Consular officers also work on humanitarian cases, which Don sees as one of the most satisfying aspects of his job. One example is the consulate's partnership with a foundation similar to "Make a Wish," facilitating travel for terminally ill children who want to visit Disneyland or somewhere else in the U.S.

Don joined the Foreign Service in 1992, following four years of overseas work, first as managing editor for the American Chamber of Commerce in Korea, and then as the director of the American Medical Center in Moscow. He has served in Ciudad Juarez, Mexico; Seoul, Korea; and Bogota, Colombia. He was born in Rapid City, South Dakota. He has a B.A. in international relations from Johns Hopkins University, and an M.A. from Johns Hopkins School of Advanced International Studies. He and his wife, Eugenia, have two young children.

Public Affairs Officer
SHARON HUDSON-DEAN
EMBASSY TBILISI, GEORGIA

The public affairs section manages the embassy's informational and cultural programs, which support and explain official U.S. policies and actions to host country government officials, media, and citizens. A large embassy divides these responsibilities between an information officer and a cultural affairs officer, but at a smaller embassy, all public diplomacy duties fall solely to the public affairs officer (PAO). Sharon Hudson-Dean, 34, is the PAO in Tbilisi, Georgia, a small former Soviet republic nestled in the Caucasus.

Sharon introduces speakers at a Georgian Fire Department ceremony in commemoration of September 11.

As Embassy Tbilisi's representative to the media, Sharon is the only officer at post besides the ambassador who is authorized to speak directly to the press. "The U.S. government must speak clearly and with one voice on issues of key national interest," she says. By working closely with all mission sections and the ambassador, Sharon keeps on top of fast-breaking issues as well as long-term strategic American interests in Georgia and the surrounding countries. When she speaks to the media, she tries to make sure she can unequivocally explain U.S. policy on any given issue.

When wearing her cultural affairs hat, Sharon manages cultural programs that play a critical role in educating foreign citizens about the United States. While there will always be foreigners who disagree with U.S. policy and actions, Sharon explains that the U.S. government believes that they should understand why Americans think and act the way they do, rather than make false assumptions about who and what America is. Therefore, the PAO sends foreign citizens to the U.S., for both short and more extended visits, to study and meet with American professional colleagues. "When these people return to their home countries, they have a new and deeper insight into the United States, which helps them to better interpret information they receive at home about America — one of our primary goals," she says.

The public affairs section also sponsors visits for American speakers, like academics and writers, and cultural groups, such as performing artists of all varieties, to familiarize Georgian citizens with American culture. For example, in one of her proudest achievements at post, Sharon brought retired managers of the U.S. National Symphony Orchestra and the Kennedy Center to Tbilisi to teach seminars on fundraising and arts management to Georgian gallery owners and cultural institution managers.

Sharon begins her day by greeting her staff of 10 in the embassy's public affairs section, located in the ballroom of the Orbeliani Palace, the former home of an aristocratic Georgian family. She then meets with the ambassador and the deputy chief of mission to discuss international and local events about which she may receive media inquiries. She also meets with Georgian contacts who present her with proposals for and reports on cultural exchange projects.

ABKHAZIA

GREATER CAUCASUS

Sokhumi

Mt'a
Shkhara

Sea

Zugdidi

SOUTH
OSSETIA

MOUNTAINS

K'olkhet'is Dablobi

K'ut'aisi

Ts'khinvali

Pankisi
Gorge

P'oti

Sup'sa

Mtkvari

Gori

LESSER CAUCASUS

T'BILISI

AZE

Bat'umi

AJARIA

Akhalts'ikhe

Rust'avi

Akhalk'alak'i

Kur

TURKEY

AZERBAIJAN

"When exchange visitors return to their home countries, they have a new and deeper insight into the United States."

Sharon's office frequently drafts and sends out press releases on items ranging from the start of a new exchange program to the visit of a high-level official from the United States. If she anticipates that a press release will generate numerous inquiries, she will schedule a press conference or one-on-one interview with the ambassador or herself. She will then direct her staff to draft and send to Washington a transcript of the interview and a summary of how the Georgian press covered the media event. A typical day also includes a visit to a partner institution, such as a university or media outlet, either to give a presentation or to make arrangements for a visit by the ambassador.

For a PAO, the day seldom ends when the sun sets. Several times a week, Sharon attends evening events such as receptions or concerts. Three or four times a month she hosts a dinner or reception at her home or at a local restaurant to honor an American visitor or celebrate the start or conclusion of one of her programs.

According to Sharon, a public affairs officer must like talking to people — giving media interviews and lectures and conducting meetings. The best PAOs, she emphasizes, have a keen ability to understand their audiences, what their predispositions are, how best to engage them. While calling PAO duties "the fun work of an embassy," Sharon stresses that a PAO must also be good at more mundane tasks like managing programs, budgets, and personnel. Sharon believes that taking care of her people and investing training in them pay off in high morale and a true team spirit. "Above all," says Sharon, "attention to detail is key for a public affairs officer." One area where even the smallest detail is important is protocol. "A U.S. ambassador is the personal representative of the president, so when I make arrangements for a visit or speech by the ambassador, every aspect of the event must run smoothly and reflect positively on the government and people of the United States."

Sharon during an interview with Reuters TV.

Sharon received her bachelor's degree from Georgetown University's School of Foreign Service. She completed one year of graduate study at the Monterey Institute of International Studies before joining the United States Information Agency in 1993. Her previous assignments have included Canberra and Sydney, Australia; and Moscow, Russia. Her hometown is Allentown, Pennsylvania. Sharon is part of a tandem couple. Her husband, Nick Dean, is the political/economic section chief at Embassy Tbilisi. They have a 3-year-old son.

Law Enforcement Coordinator and Narcotics Affairs Counselor

Jim with office management specialist Isabel Kuver at USEU.

JIM WAGNER
U.S. MISSION TO THE EUROPEAN UNION, BRUSSELS, BELGIUM

Fighting international crime was not a key priority for U.S. embassies until the 1990s, when it became clear to foreign policy managers that international crime had advanced well beyond country-by-country tracking of fugitives across borders. The rise of the Internet, for example, led to a new reality in which criminals could commit international crimes without leaving their computer terminals, let alone their countries. The Internet has made crime today effectively borderless, explains Jim Wagner, the narcotics affairs counselor and law enforcement coordinator (LEC) at the U.S. Mission to the European Union.

The job of the narcotics affairs counselor in Brussels is to be the bridge between the U.S. and the European Union on criminal judicial issues and counternarcotics programs and policies. Jim, 45, advocates U.S. interests before the "ever-evolving" E.U. For law enforcement that means laying a solid foundation for working with newly emerging E.U. institutions and soon-to-be centralized criminal judicial decision-making within the E.U. "Perhaps the biggest challenge for me and my colleague from the Justice Department's Criminal Division," says Jim, "has been to anticipate the impact on the U.S. ability to fight international crime from the evolution taking place within the E.U."

To ensure that the expanding anti-crime activities in overseas missions were being conducted in the most effective manner possible, and to ensure that U.S. foreign policy interests were maintained in the activities conducted by law enforcement officials, over the past decade embassies and missions have been instructed to create law enforcement committees. These committees include representatives from all law enforcement elements at post and are chaired by the deputy chief of mission or the ambassador. Members often include representatives from the FBI, the Justice Department, the Drug Enforcement Administration, the Secret Service, and the Immigration and Naturalization Service. The law enforcement coordinator manages the committee. The LEC position is not full-time, and the Foreign Service officer in the position has other, often related, responsibilities.

Jim Wagner often compares his job to that of the policeman directing traffic at a busy intersection. "Like the cop, I need to know who is coming in each direction, where they

"Our work is tricky, somewhat like being the uninvited guest at the party. We don't have access to the inner workings of the E.U., but the U.S. is potentially impacted by most E.U. decisions."

intend to go and when I can expect the incoming traffic to arrive." He must keep U.S. government actions flowing efficiently and effectively. The difference is that he watches criminals and tracks the law enforcement efforts to combat them.

The U.S. Mission to the European Union serves as the representative of the U.S. government before the E.U. The 15 current member states are Austria, Belgium, Denmark, Finland, France, Germany, Greece, Ireland, Italy, Luxembourg, Netherlands, Portugal, Spain, Sweden, and the United Kingdom. The E.U. is scheduled to significantly expand membership in 2004. Since the U.S. is not a member of the European Union, that "makes us the outsiders," Jim explains. "Our work is tricky, somewhat like being the uninvited guest at the party. We don't have access to the inner workings of the E.U., but the U.S. is potentially impacted by most E.U. decisions."

The U.S. has good relations with each member state of the European Union, but as the E.U. increasingly centralizes police and judicial systems, there will be a need to reconfigure each bilateral relationship as well. "We at USEU are working today to develop appropriate links with the new E.U. institutions and officials," says Jim, "to help smooth the way into this new and uncharted area of U.S.-E.U. criminal judicial cooperation."

Just after the terrorist attacks of September 11, Jim was invited to meet with European law enforcement terrorism experts. In the immediate aftermath of the attacks, he could not expect detailed input from Washington for his meeting with E.U. officials. "We at the U.S. mission developed the agenda based on our knowledge, our experience, and our expertise," he recalls. "That is what Foreign Service officers do every day — apply knowledge and skills to the promotion of U.S. interests." That meeting led to further cooperation, and one of the results has been a cooperative agreement between the U.S. and the European Police Office, signed in December 2001 in the presence of Secretary of State Colin Powell and the justice and interior ministers of all the E.U. member states. It underscored the growing link between criminal/judicial and foreign policy interests, with the ultimate goal, as Jim puts it, of "making all our societies safe from crime."

Jim Wagner joined the Foreign Service fresh out of graduate school in 1981. He has a B.A. in international studies from Otterbein College and an M.S. from the School of Foreign Service at Georgetown University. His Foreign Service assignments have included Managua, Nicaragua; Madrid, Spain; Washington, D.C.; Cebu, Philippines; Maracaibo, Venezuela; and Lima, Peru. He is married to Ruth Villavicencio, who received the American Foreign Service Association's Avis Bohlen Award for community service during their tour in Venezuela. They have three children, one of whom received the Foreign Service Youth Award from the Foreign Service Youth Foundation in 2001.

Refugee Coordinator
RANDY BERRY
EMBASSY KAMPALA, UGANDA

The job of a refugee coordinator is to track, analyze, and report on refugee movements and the situations that produce them, as well as assess needs and evaluate activities and interventions funded by the U.S. government. The refugee coordinator also plays a key role in alerting Washington to emerging crises in the region and suggesting ways the U.S. government might intervene to improve conditions for or protection of refugees.

Randy Berry, 37, serves as the regional refugee coordinator for the Great Lakes and Central Africa region. He is based at a Embassy Kampala, a medium-size post in East Africa. There are about 55 American employees at the embassy — including representatives of the State Department, USAID, the Peace Corps, the Centers for Disease Control, and the Defense Department — and 320 Ugandan employees. Randy travels 30 to 35 percent of the time, covering refugee affairs in Uganda, Rwanda, Burundi, Tanzania, Democratic Republic of Congo, Republic of Congo, Gabon, and the Central African Republic. Armed conflict, natural disasters, and minimal infrastructure all contribute to making the region an especially challenging one in which to live and work.

The refugee coordinator serves as the primary field link between the U.S. government and international and local organizations supporting refugee work. Refugee coordinator positions are supported by the State Department's Bureau of Population, Refugees and Migration. Randy liaises directly with a number of United Nations agencies (most often the U.N. High Commission for Refugees, known as UNHCR), the International Committee of the Red Cross (ICRC), the national Red Cross/Red Crescent Societies, and international and local non-governmental organizations (NGOs) involved with humanitarian work. In most cases, he works with each of these groups in several different countries. Randy monitors implementation of projects funded by the Bureau of Population, Refugees, and Migration, which are carried out by UNHCR, ICRC, and NGOs in the region. In each of the countries in his region, Randy also works with government officials on policy issues and on protection and assistance to refugee communities.

"Nobody enjoys life as a refugee," Randy explains. "It is an extremely difficult, harsh, and bewildering experience." The aim of U.S. government refugee assistance is to find ways to help people live with greater dignity and pride, even in a temporary refugee camp. "By providing the means to access clean water, a school, a micro-loan to start a small business, or by providing tools and seeds to allow refugees to care for themselves more independently, we enable them to regain greater control over their own lives," says Randy.

When Randy is in the field, he spends much of his time assessing conditions in refugee camps and settlements. The focus is usually on key issues such as water and sanitation, health care, and sexual and gender-based violence prevention education. During one trip through Tanzania, Randy observed a repatriation under way of Burundians returning

The refugee coordinator serves as the primary field link between the U.S. government and international and local organizations supporting refugee work.

home from Tanzania; visited a soap-making cooperative founded and run by refugees; and monitored a U.S. government-funded gender-based violence drop-in center in the Kitali Hills Refugee Camp in Ngara, where victims of violence can come for medical care, counseling, legal rights information, and access to psychological support. Randy also spends a lot of time talking about clean water and latrines — key issues in refugee camps — and thinks he probably knows more about the various types of latrines than most other Foreign Service officers.

Meeting the people who live and work in or near refugee camps has been a highlight of Randy's work as a refugee coordinator. He has been awed by the heavy burden of work that African refugee women bear, and sees support for the efforts to strengthen refugee women's abilities to care for their families as one of the most significant contributions made by the State Department's refugee program in his region.

When he is in the capitals of the countries he covers, Randy meets with numerous international and local organizations, as well as government representatives, to obtain briefings and information on humanitarian programs. When he is in Kampala, he spends much time going over the vast amount of information he has collected during monitoring trips, maintains e-mail contact with people he works with in the field, writes detailed monitoring and evaluation reports, and reviews project proposals and makes recommendations for or against funding. Randy also manages to remain part of mission life by serving as the embassy's housing board chairman and Equal Employment Opportunity officer, and fill-

Visiting the Agago Primary School at Achol-pii Refugee Camp for Sudanese in northern Uganda.

ing in as a consular officer. He even spent three months as the acting deputy chief of mission.

Prior to joining the Foreign Service, Randy was an in-flight safety instructor for America West Airlines. He has a B.A. in education from Bethany College, and pursued M.A. coursework in art history at the University of Adelaide. He grew up in Custer County, Colorado. Randy joined the Foreign Service in 1993, and has served in Dhaka, Bangladesh; Cairo, Egypt; and back-to-back tours in Kampala, first as a political officer and then as refugee coordinator. His next assignment is in Washington as a country desk officer for South Africa.

Labor Officer
JOHN W. CHAMBERLIN
EMBASSY BEIJING, CHINA

The labor officer is one of those few people in an embassy who bridges the political and economic worlds, working in the area where the interests and activities of the host country's government, employers, and employees converge. "Understanding this point of convergence helps us understand and influence significant human rights issues, the political and economic situation in the country, and the prospects for economic growth and stability," explains Embassy Beijing's labor officer, John Chamberlin.

The labor officer reports on labor-related developments in the host country, represents official U.S. positions on labor issues to the host government and other interested parties and, where relevant, coordinates U.S. government cooperative labor programs.

The State Department has labor officers at key embassies around the world, often based in the political section. In Beijing, the labor officer is part of the economic section, working closely with the political section, especially the human rights officer. John, 60, is one of 14 officers in the economic section. He coordinates labor reporting with officers at the other China posts: Guangzhou, Shenyang, Shanghai and Chengdu.

Like all labor officers, John has two key Washington constituencies: the State Department and the Department of Labor. He also works closely with the Treasury Department, especially through the U.S. Customs attaché at the embassy, on questions of prison labor and child labor. In addition, he is in regular contact with non-governmental human rights groups and international organizations, as well as business representatives.

Labor issues in China are unusually complex, affected by the massive economic change from a planned economy to a free market economy. Workers in old industries are losing jobs. Millions of Chinese peasants, hit hard by economic upheaval, are migrating to cities to find work. How the population adjusts to these wrenching changes, and how government and business respond, will have a powerful impact on China's economic development and political stability.

In this context, the key issues for John include worker rights and the establishment and enforcement of core labor standards; rising unemployment and the development of a social safety net and programs to assist workers find new jobs; the social challenge posed by the growing migrant labor population; the development and enforcement of an effective system of labor laws and regulations to advance the rule of law; and the prevention of the export to the U.S. of goods made by prisoners, children, or forced labor. Through analysis and reporting, John tries to provide U.S. policy-makers with a broad yet incisive view of the labor situation in China. The job involves more than reporting, however, and includes planning programs that could provide U.S. technical assistance to China in developing and enforcing labor laws and improving worker safety.

"We can help China see that everyone's interest in a stable global trading system will be undermined if workers are not treated fairly."

Another important facet of John's job is to promote the protection of workers' rights in China, which he sees as consistent with advancing U.S. trade and investment interests and promoting global trade. China's enormous labor supply, its low wages, and inconsistent application of worker protections attract more and more investment looking for low production costs. This "race to the bottom" affects jobs, wages, and workplace standards in developing countries and even in the U.S. "With China's entry into the World Trade Organization and its recognition that it needs to adopt laws and practices consistent with international norms, we can help China see that everyone's interest in a stable global trading system will be undermined if workers are not treated fairly," John says.

John travels outside Beijing about 15 percent of the time, meeting with officials, talking with workers and employers at factories and mines, and visiting prisons. When he's in Beijing, he often checks in with colleagues in the Customs office about prison labor issues and with the political section's human rights officer about worker rights cases or rule of law programs. John regularly sees officials at the Chinese Ministry of Labor and Social Security and the State Administration for Work Safety to discuss U.S.-China labor program planning and coordinate the increasing tempo of official visits. Most days include work on labor reporting cables and usually close with e-mails to the Department of Labor and the State Department's China Desk and Bureau of Democracy, Human Rights and Labor, among other key constituents. Because of the 12-hour time difference, these messages are received at opening of business in Washington.

Before taking the Beijing position, John had served primarily in political jobs and had not considered working in labor affairs. "I have found this job to be one of the most stimulating, and toughest, I've done in the Foreign Service," he says. "It is fascinating to observe a country in such transition, especially where major forces of economic and social — and potentially political — change come together in the lives of hundreds of millions of working people."

Before joining the Foreign Service in 1980, John was a university professor. He has served in Kuwait City, Kuwait; Abu Dhabi, United Arab Emirates; Tel Aviv, Israel; Singapore; the Air Force Academy in Colorado Springs, Colorado; and Washington, D.C. He grew up in Syracuse, New York, and has a B.A. in English from Dartmouth College and a Ph.D. from Columbia University in international relations. He served in Nigeria as a Peace Corps volunteer. He and his wife, Martha, have two grown daughters.

Environmental Officer

RICHARD S. D. HAWKINS
EMBASSY ABIDJAN, COTE D'IVOIRE

Environmental issues have become increasingly critical over time as the world's population increases while resources are depleted and degraded. As more land is opened up to logging, hunting, and mineral exploration, as fishing activities and pollution put stress on ocean wildlife, and as natural and manmade processes reduce rainfall and expand desert areas in many parts of the world, disagreements between people and nations over the appropriate balance between man and nature have become sharper. Nearly all environmental issues have physical, economic, and social consequences.

Because environmental problems transcend national borders, the State Department's Bureau of Oceans and International Environmental and Scientific Affairs (OES) established regional environmental hubs, located in 12 embassies around the world. Each hub office is run by a regional environmental officer (REO), whose role is to look at environmental issues from a region-wide perspective. The REO complements the activities of the traditional environment, science, and technology officers in many embassies, who are focused on bilateral issues. The REO engages with the countries in the region in an effort to promote environmental cooperation, sharing of data, and adoption of environmentally sound policies that can benefit all the countries of the region.

Discussing Bocanda reforestation project at a village field site.

"The key challenge for the REO," says Dick Hawkins, the regional environmental officer at Embassy Abidjan in Cote d'Ivoire, "is to determine the critical, fundamental environmental issues in the region and to look for ways to move those issues in directions that will be positive for the local populations and for the U.S." The regional environmental officers serve as advisors to U.S. embassies on environmental policies and developments relevant to U.S. foreign policy objectives. They often represent the U.S. government in regional activities and sometimes negotiate agreements on behalf of the U.S. They also design, propose, and administer transboundary projects to advance environmental understanding and policy development.

Dick, 59, covers the vast Western and Central African regions, which run from Cape Verde and Western Sahara through Chad down to the Democratic Republic of the Congo. Embassy Abidjan is a large regional hub, where more than 12 agencies are represented. There are 86 American Foreign Service employees at the embassy, and about 420 Foreign Service Nationals. Dick reports to the political/economic counselor but receives instructions from the OES Bureau and his budget from the Bureau of African Affairs.

The REO's responsibilities span many issues, with security, political, and economic implications. For example, Dick looks for ways to avert conflict and violence over control

of diminishing African natural resources, especially over potable water and arable land.

There is a humanitarian element to his job, as he works to support programs to alleviate suffering caused by environmental degradation and related threats to health and welfare, and to facilitate American assistance and technical support. On the political front, he must always be ready to explain U.S. environmental policy to occasionally skeptical audiences. And in economic matters, he seeks to gain advantage for U.S. trade and investment, especially where Africa's many agricultural and extractive industries are concerned.

The regional environmental officer is often on the move. Dick travels between 10 and 40 percent of the time, depending on the time of year, working out of the U.S. embassies in the countries he covers. Travel in Western and Central Africa is difficult and unreliable, and visits to small embassies in the region must be carefully planned so as not to strain their limited resources. On the road and at home in Abidjan, Dick spends his time coordinating with international organizations, government officials in each country, non-governmental organizations, and the private sector. He also works with other U.S. government agencies — including USAID, the Environmental Protection Agency, the U.S. Department of Agriculture, the Foreign Commercial Service, and the Peace Corps — on development and implementation of environmental policy initiatives in the region.

Dick was able to draw U.S. government attention to the region's serious fresh water supply problems, particularly the importance and degraded status of the great Senegal, Gambia, Niger, Volta, and Congo River basins and Lake Chad. He won funding from the department for cooperative projects to help alleviate the problems. He also drew international attention to the link between Liberian President Charles Taylor's sponsorship of unsustainable logging practices and his importation of weapons to help rebels destabilize Sierra Leone and Guinea.

Dick came later in life to the Foreign Service, leaving a successful career in the private sector to join an entering class of diplomats at age 52. He has a B.A. in English from Harvard University, an M.A. in Southeast Asia studies from Yale University, and an M.S. in international business from Rensselaer Polytechnic Institute in Troy, New York. He co-founded an educational publishing house in Cambridge, Massachusetts, and subsequently worked for a variety of large multinational corporations. Hawkins married Foreign Service officer Patricia McMahon Hawkins in 1989 and joined the Foreign Service in 1995. They have two children from previous marriages. He served for four years in Abidjan, first as a political officer and then as Abidjan's first regional environment officer. He has also served in Bogota, Colombia. His next assignment is to Santo Domingo, Dominican Republic.

Management Officer
Tulinabo S. Mushingi
CONSULATE GENERAL CASABLANCA, MOROCCO

Every organization — from a large company to a small non-profit — needs a business manager to oversee its day-to-day operations. United States embassies and consulates are no exception. Tulinabo (Tuli) Mushingi, 46, serves as management officer — the business manager — for the U.S. consulate general in Casablanca, a bustling port city on Morocco's Atlantic coast.

As management officer, Tuli has a variety of duties, ranging from overseeing the consulate's human resources section to procuring maintenance, travel, and transportation services for the 15 American and 40 local employees at post. He also manages a portion of the $5 million annual budget allocated between the consulate and the embassy in Rabat. As financial officer, Tuli pays the bills and makes recommendations for budget cuts and increases directly to the consul general. He is also responsible for the consulate's computer and communications systems. His work in these areas has focused on making the consulate a more paper-free environment and instituting the "international voice gateway," a phone line that will save the consulate tens of thousands of dollars per year.

A management officer (previously known as administrative officer) is also responsible for finding appropriate housing for the mission's American employees. Tuli considers many factors when buying or leasing houses and apartments, including safety, security, family size, and the amount of representational entertaining the officers' particular jobs require. He also oversees his post's health unit and community liaison office and is the consulate's representative on the board of the Casablanca American School. These issues are of particular importance to the morale and sense of well-being at any post.

Since Consulate General Casablanca is a relatively small post, Tuli also serves as the mission's security officer. He manages security issues for the consulate building, the consul general's residence, the annex building housing the public affairs section, and 15 leased employee residences. To ensure the consulate's security, Tuli supervises the local guard force and maintains close ties with Casablanca's law-enforcement officials.

A typical day begins with a review of the consulate's security posture. On his way to work, he greets the local guards and police posted outside the consulate. He then meets with his staff and reviews the day's work goals with his assistant. At his desk, Tuli checks his e-mail messages for the most pressing requests from the consulate community, Embassy Rabat and Washington. Throughout the day, he takes action on work and travel orders, negotiates vendor contracts, and pays the bills. Later in the day he visits other sections of the consulate, including the classified access areas. At least once a day, Tuli touches base with Embassy Rabat, to coordinate expenditures, personnel, and regional issues.

> Unlike some of the more policy-related jobs, where results are seen sometimes after months, years or even decades, the management officer is able to point to numerous concrete accomplishments literally every day.

Tuli defines his role as that of providing support to the mission so that other sections can easily and comfortably perform their jobs. If members of the consulate community are worried about their housing, health care, work conditions, or other aspects of life at post, they will not be able to focus on the foreign policy mission of the consulate. In other words, in any country the post's effectiveness depends heavily on its management officer.

Management officers have to be flexible enough to deal with whatever situations arise, according to Tuli. If a high-level official such as the Secretary of State announces a visit to post, the management officer must quickly redirect the efforts of his staff to prepare for the visit. The management officer himself will play a key role in coordinating the visit, making sure everything from security to transportation runs as smoothly as possible. Likewise, international events often influence the management officer's day-to-day duties. Since September 11, for example, Tuli has focused his efforts on increasing consulate employees' familiarity with emergency procedures. He even spent several days supervising the conversion of an empty shipping container into a temporary mailroom in the aftermath of several anthrax scares at the consulate.

Tuli says his job is satisfying because "it provides so many opportunities to make a positive impact on the everyday life of the mission community." Unlike some of the more policy-related jobs, Tuli notes, where results are seen sometimes after months, years or even decades, the management officer is able to point to numerous concrete accomplishments

Seeing Secretary of State Colin Powell off in Casablanca.

literally every day, an aspect of his job that he finds particularly fulfilling.

Following a career of university teaching and work for the Peace Corps, Tuli joined the State Department in 1989 and the Foreign Service in 1991. He holds a Ph.D. in linguistics from Georgetown University and a master's degree in linguistics and French from Howard University. He also holds undergraduate degrees in French and African literature and linguistics from the National University of Zaire (now the Democratic Republic of the Congo). His previous Foreign Service assignments have included Kuala Lumpur, Malaysia; Maputo, Mozambique; and Washington, D.C. Tuli was born in the Democratic Republic of Congo and became a naturalized U.S. citizen in the early eighties. He and his wife, Rebecca, have a teen-age daughter.

Security Officer
KIM T. STARKE
EMBASSY MANILA, PHILIPPINES

Embassy Manila is a large mission facing multiple security threats requiring numerous and varied responses, all of which are Kim Starke's responsibility as the embassy's security officer (formally called regional security officer, or RSO). There are frequent demonstrations outside the embassy and terrorist threats to the embassy, and the Philippines is always at risk for earthquakes, typhoons, and other natural disasters. Kim manages the embassy's security program for the ambassador, who is ultimately responsible for the safety of all official Americans in the Philippines and in the small country of Palau. He also handles all security issues for the U.S. embassies in Kolonia, Micronesia and Majuro, Marshall Islands.

Kim with a local guard at an Embassy Manila construction site.

Although many people think security officers must have a background in law enforcement or intelligence, Kim says the key requirements are good managerial and administrative skills and a keen interest in working with others. The security officer has to be flexible and responsive in what can be a swiftly changing environment. With the increasing threat of terrorism has come an increased awareness for all security officers worldwide that no post is truly secure, and even embassies in "low threat" countries can become targets for terrorists.

Kim, 50, supervises four assistant security officers, a seven-person Marine security guard detachment, a security engineering office staff of eight, 250 locally hired guards for embassy compound and residential security, seven local investigators, and a 12-person protective detail for the ambassador, as well as a 12-person surveillance detection staff.

"I'm here to ensure that our diplomats are safe both at work and in their homes so they can carry out the business of diplomacy," says Kim. His primary areas of concern are personal, procedural, residential, and technical security. He is responsible for protecting classified information from human and technical threats, and for creating and maintaining a secure work environment for the processing and discussion of classified information.

The security officer plays a pivotal role in managing the embassy's Emergency Action Plan, a document each embassy must have in place in preparation for response to potential crises, from terrorist attacks to natural disasters. The security officer makes sure all employees know what their responsibilities are in the event of an emergency and are prepared — through training and drills — to carry them out.

The security officer at an embassy or consulate is never completely off duty, unless he is out of the country. There is a duty officer on call 24 hours a day at every U.S. embassy, and in the case of an emergency after hours, that person always knows how to reach the security officer. The RSO may be contacted when Washington offices need security updates on

> No post is truly secure, and even embassies in "low threat" countries can become targets for terrorists.

local situations, when an embassy employee or family member is involved in a vehicle accident, and for any other security-related event. In addition, private Americans often require assistance at all hours of the day and night.

A typical day starts with a review of intelligence reports that may have an impact on the mission or the situation in the Philippines in general. Kim then routinely briefs the ambassador and the deputy chief of mission on current security concerns, and alerts them to security-related issues that might arise in their contacts with local government officials.

He spends much of his day maintaining contact with various local law enforcement personnel, especially the local police. A Philippine national police special action force consisting of 27 heavily armed and well-trained Philippine police officers helps guard the embassy compound. Improving the preparedness of local law enforcement is another way to help improve the security environment for all resident Americans. Kim has helped organize security-training opportunities for over 300 local police officers, senators, prosecutors and other officials. Embassy Manila supports an active Anti-Terrorism Assistance Program, which is run by the State Department's Diplomatic Security Service. Kim also manages the Rewards for Justice Program in the Philippines. This program has rewards of up to $5 million for information that leads to the arrest or conviction of leaders of the Abu Sayyaf group in the Philippines.

Kim frequently meets with members of the American community living in the Philippines, who are not part of the official U.S. mission, to brief them on the local security situation. He has helped create a new Overseas Security Advisory Council in Manila, which gathers American business representatives together to exchange security concerns and seek solutions.

Kim consults with a Marine security guard.

Kim joined the Foreign Service in 1977, and has served as a security officer in Mogadishu, Somalia; Gaborone, Botswana; Canberra, Australia; and Nairobi, Kenya. He has also done several tours in the U.S., including a stint as a special agent on the secretary of State's protective detail and as the special agent in charge of Diplomatic Security's Chicago field office. He has a B.S. in criminal justice from the University of Wisconsin at Platteville and an M.A. in police science and administration from Washington State University. He and his wife, Virginia, have three children.

Information Management Officer

MIKE KOVICH
EMBASSY MEXICO CITY, MEXICO

Information Management Officer Mike Kovich runs the office that supports the information and communications operations of over 1,700 people employed by 35 U.S. government agencies based at Embassy Mexico City and the nine consulates and 13 consular agencies throughout Mexico. He must understand and support all the different

technologies and communication systems utilized by all U.S. government agencies with missions in Mexico. It is a big job, but one that Mike, 55, would not trade for any other.

The information management officer (IMO) serves as the Department of State's senior information management professional at the embassy where he or she serves. The IMO provides management oversight and operational control of classified and unclassified information technology for all the posts in his country of assignment. This includes management of international satellite and leased line operations; classified and unclassified data processing; telephone systems in the embassies and consulates; radio systems; videoconferencing systems; mail operations, both regular and diplomatic pouch; local area network administration; and technology training. The IMO also serves as the U.S. government's representative and resident expert on communications issues, and liaises with other U.S. government agencies in-country as well as the host country's ministry of communications.

Embassy Mexico City's information resources management office is staffed by 14 Foreign Service information management specialists and 36 Foreign Service National employees. Mike strives to maintain a working environment that promotes motivation, participation, and professional development of the communications staff. He is a strong advocate of training, and Embassy Mexico City hosts computer training workshops for American and Mexican employees.

Mike is in frequent contact with all nine U.S. consulates in Mexico on a variety of security and communications issues. Regular days at work include handling one or more "brush fires," he says, "issues that must be addressed and resolved immediately before they get out of hand."

Another key responsibility of the IMO is ensuring that VIP visits to Mexico run smoothly. He has to establish and support unique communications needs for presidential and other high-level visits. Mike recently traveled to Los Cabos, Mexico, for instance, to meet with the presidential pre-advance team to discuss requirements for an upcoming presidential visit to that city. He met with Mexican counterparts several times before the visit to facilitate the expansion of the technical infrastructure in Los Cabos to support the visit.

Mike is also leading the new Foreign Affairs Systems Integration pilot project designed to establish a common platform to manage and facilitate information sharing among U.S. government agencies with a presence overseas. The objective is to permit all U.S. government agencies to communicate and share information from their desktops, regardless of their location. The demands of the project have placed a heavy burden on the information management staff, but Mike says they are proud to be leading this initiative that could be destined for worldwide use.

The IMO must be flexible and versatile, and can be called upon to occupy other positions in the embassy as needs arise. Mike has filled in for the minister counselor for administrative affairs, and learned from that experience that "you must establish your own credibility, and then there is no limit to where your achievements may lead you." He ensures that his staff gain experience in a wide range of assignments so they can be ready to perform any function within the information management arena. He sees his greatest achievement as serving as a mentor and helping his staff gain versatility they can take with them to future assignments.

Most days begin with a check on the status of communications operations at the embassy and the nine consulates. After that, Mike usually meets with his staff, reviews outstanding issues on the classified networks and reviews incoming telegrams. He also gives a briefing to the administrative counselor. No two days are alike, and he might next plan the installation of a new project, handle a personnel issue, or coordinate with counterparts from other agencies. Mike views his experience in the Foreign Service as "a true adventure" that could not be matched by any private sector job. "Where else could you work face-to-face with the secretary of State?" he asks. His spirit of adventure drew him to the more unusual and challenging postings, including Moscow during the Cold War and Afghanistan after the Soviet invasion.

Independence Day in Mexico City.

Mike joined the Foreign Service in 1977, following a seven-year career as a communications technician for the U.S. Navy in Iceland and Southeast Asia. His Foreign Service assignments have included Buenos Aires, Argentina; Moscow, then-USSR; Kabul, Afghanistan; Santo Domingo, Dominican Republic; Asuncion, Paraguay; Guatemala City, Guatemala; Bogota, Colombia; and Washington, D.C. In addition, he did a three-year tour as an African rover, serving as a troubleshooter in many hardship posts in Africa. Mike was raised in the small farming community of Owosso, Michigan, and is the single father of two sons.

Office Management Specialist
CONNIE PARISH
EMBASSY SARAJEVO, BOSNIA AND HERZEGOVINA

Office management specialists are the glue that holds an embassy together. "The office management specialist (OMS) is vital to the overall function and well-being of an embassy, and serves as the communications hub for the office in which she works," says Connie Parish, the OMS for the ambassador in Sarajevo.

On any given day, the OMS may be preparing a demarche or a diplomatic note for the ambassador, greeting high-level visitors on the airport tarmac, arranging high-level meet-

Connie (seated) with Ambassador Cliff Bond (left), OMS Sue Rowell and Deputy Chief of Mission Chris Hoh.

ings for embassy staff or visitors, planning a reception at the ambassador's residence, ordering supplies, and escorting local cleaning or work crews to secure areas. Above all, the OMS must be flexible, innovative and adaptive, always ready to step in and handle any task. Life at an embassy is ever-changing, and the OMS must keep operations going smoothly in occasionally chaotic or fluid situations.

Connie Parish, 52, is the senior OMS at Embassy Sarajevo, a 660-person embassy. Bosnia is still emerging from a devastating four-year war, and ethnic tensions are always just beneath the surface waiting to erupt. Connie manages the ambassador's office, called "the front office." Security threats, such as two terrorist threats to Embassy Sarajevo resulting in brief embassy shutdowns in 2001 and 2002, have created extra coordination requirements for her, as well as longer hours.

As the ambassador's OMS, Connie must always be aware of the rapidly changing political situation, as well as the broader security situation. She has to be able to identify people the ambassador may need to see quickly, as well as those who can wait. This kind of knowledge cannot be found in any manual. It comes from experience and from being a quick study. The ambassador's office is inundated with information and requests; the OMS has the critical role of sorting it all out so that the ambassador is able to focus on the right issues and tasks.

The OMS is usually "in the eye of the storm," as Connie puts it, and serves as the focal point for general information for the whole embassy. Although some of the tasks may seem mundane, Connie sees each as a piece of a bigger picture. "The OMS is a vital link in helping deliver the president's messages to the world, whether it's good news or bad," she says.

Connie is highly involved with the operation of the ambassador's residence. She helps train household staff, oversees the running of events, manages guest lists and menus and ensures that the house is in perfect working order. "I have developed a rapport with the ambassador and he relies on me to communicate accurately his wishes to the entire

The ambassador's office is inundated with requests; the OMS has the critical role of sorting it all out so that the ambassador is able to focus on the right issues and tasks.

embassy and residence staff," she says.

There are no typical days in Sarajevo. Connie arrives at work at 7:15 a.m., greets the Marine guard, and, using several different lock combinations, enters her office. She sets up the office, opens safes, brings the language teacher to the ambassador's office, and prepares the papers the ambassador will need that day. Then she goes over e-mails and cable traffic. During the workday, she greets visitors, sets up appointments, tracks the paper flow, and updates the ambassador's schedule. While he's in meetings, she's "in constant motion coordinating a myriad of issues with the deputy chief of mission's secretary, other missions in Sarajevo, residence staff, other embassy offices, the ambassador's bodyguards, and the ambassador himself," she says. The ambassador will often call Connie from his car between appointments to check on the status of a meeting request or fast-breaking news.

Among her other tasks, Connie helps supervise the four-person protocol office. She also manages classified files and ensures that security regulations are followed. She must maintain good relations with local government officials as well as international business and diplomatic contacts. At about 5 p.m., she prepares a folder for the ambassador for the following day's events, and uses this "quiet time" to do paperwork, return phone calls, and answer e-mails. After the ambassador leaves for the evening, usually around 7 p.m., she secures his office and goes home.

"I have been in the Foreign Service for 15 years and absolutely, unequivocally love my job," Connie says. "An OMS position with the Foreign Service can be exciting and rewarding, but it's not for everyone," she adds. "You have to be ready to go anywhere, and must be highly self-reliant."

Connie is from Clearwater, Florida. Her pre-Foreign Service life included sewing work in

Connie and fellow OMS Rosalie Kahn at the site of the Mostar bridge.

the tobacco sheds of the American Sumatra Tobacco Company as a high school student, followed by seven years as a long distance operator for General Telephone. She lived around the world with her Air Force husband, and raised three children. She joined the Foreign Service in 1987, and has been posted to Buenos Aires, Argentina; Tegucigalpa, Honduras; Mexico City, Mexico; Bucharest, Romania (her first posting as an ambassador's OMS, and where she also served as administrative coordinator for the opening of the U.S. office in Cluj, Romania); Bonn, Germany; Sarajevo, Bosnia (following the signing of the Dayton Accords); Bogota, Colombia; Warsaw, Poland; and again in Sarajevo.

Medical Officer
BROOKS A. TAYLOR
EMBASSY NEW DELHI, INDIA

"From a medical point of view, as a family physician in the Foreign Service, much of what you see in the patient population is the same in New Delhi as it would be in Des Moines," says Dr. Brooks Taylor, regional medical officer for Embassy New Delhi, "except that Delhi is a very unhealthy place to live." New Delhi is one of the most pol-

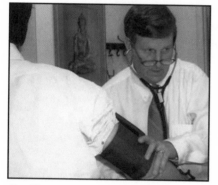

Checking a patient's blood pressure at Embassy New Delhi Medical Unit.

luted cities in the world, and air pollution causes respiratory problems for many resident Americans. Disabling diarrhea, also known as "Delhi belly," is a constant threat. The Embassy New Delhi health unit staff spend a lot of time teaching people how to reduce health risks from local food and water, and how to avoid diseases common to the area, such as typhoid, dengue fever, salmonella, rabies, and malaria.

Providing primary health care overseas gives Foreign Service medical practitioners — physicians, nurse practitioners and physician's assistants, psychiatrists, and medical technologists — unique challenges and opportunities, and affords their patients unique benefits. Brooks, 49, tells us that "the wonderful thing about practicing medicine in the Foreign Service is that I don't have to charge patients and I can see them the day they call for an appointment or immediately for an emergency, and I can spend as much time as I need to with any patient. Those things are unheard of in the managed-care milieu of the States."

There are about 29 regional medical officers (called RMOs) and about 54 Foreign Service health practitioners and physician's assistants posted overseas. In addition, there are 12 regional psychiatrists and nine regional medical technologists posted overseas. At some large embassies, several practitioners are co-located. Embassy New Delhi has one of the largest and busiest health units in the Foreign Service, with five Foreign Service medical personnel on staff: two RMOs, one psychiatrist, one medical technologist (who runs the health unit laboratory), and one health practitioner. In addition, the unit has three part-time nurses, a full-time Foreign Service National pharmacist (the only one in the Foreign Service), and four other FSN employees.

Embassy and consulate health units vary from post to post, depending on the size of the mission, the local medical capabilities, and the needs of the community. Many embassies have Foreign Service health practitioners practicing solo. Other smaller embassies have only a locally hired nurse in their health unit. A few embassies hire local physicians on contract to see patients in the health unit. The RMO supervises all the practitioners serving U.S. missions in the region and ensures the quality of care provided.

The RMO manages the entire medical program in his or her region for the Department

"The wonderful thing about practicing medicine in the Foreign Service is that I don't have to charge patients, and I can spend as much time as I need to with any patient."

of State, including efforts to maintain a healthy workforce by focusing on preventive health care through community education and periodic health screening exams. The RMO also facilitates and oversees the medical care patients receive from local specialists and hospitals. When a patient faces a medical problem that cannot be handled locally, the RMO authorizes and facilitates a medical evacuation to an appropriate health-care facility. There are regional medevac centers in Singapore, London, Pretoria, and Miami.

The Delhi health unit takes care of about 500 official U.S. government employees and family members, as well as 132 "unofficial" Americans — schoolteachers and USAID contractors. Embassy Delhi is staffed by almost 1,000 Foreign Service Nationals, who also have access to the health unit when they are injured or ill at work. The health unit not only covers the embassy community in New Delhi, but also the consulate communities in Mumbai, Chennai, and Calcutta and the embassy community in Colombo, Sri Lanka (although there are plans to staff Colombo with a Foreign Service medical practitioner soon). Brooks travels to each of the posts he covers every three months, and when emergencies arise. He is in almost daily contact with patients at the other posts, as well as the local health care providers there.

When he is in Delhi, Brooks usually sees walk-in patients every morning, and then sees scheduled patients. While he does have regular office hours, he is never truly off duty. He and all Foreign Service medical practitioners must be available 24 hours a day for medical service or consultations, and to arrange medevacs.

Embassy New Delhi employees and family members suffered from high stress and poor morale in 2001 and 2002, due to a number of causes, including September 11 and the war in nearby Afghanistan; the threat of nuclear war between India and Pakistan, and the subsequent authorized departure of non-emergency personnel and dependents; and management problems at post. Brooks has taught many emergency response courses at his posts for Americans and FSNs, as well as courses on chemical and biological weapons. The 2001 anthrax scare hit his region hard, as multiple envelopes containing white powder arrived at mailrooms in Delhi and Colombo. Brooks played a key role in the response to these threats, and held town meetings to discuss the situation with the community.

Brooks grew up in India, where his parents were missionaries. He now calls South Portland, Maine, home. He has a B.A. in Asian religions from Swarthmore College and an M.D. from Harvard Medical School. He joined the Foreign Service in 1992, following four years as a family physician in Eastport and then Bangor, Maine. Since joining the Foreign Service, he has served in Bridgetown, Barbados; Nairobi, Kenya; and Islamabad, Pakistan. Brooks and his wife, Betsy Dorman, an artist, have two teen-age children.

Junior Officer

DeAngela Burns-Wallace
EMBASSY PRETORIA, SOUTH AFRICA

DeAngela Burns-Wallace is a junior officer serving as the assistant information officer at Embassy Pretoria. Her responsibilities are anything but junior-level in importance, however. DeAngela, 27, serves as the deputy spokesperson for one of the largest U.S. missions in the world. She has to know U.S. policy — and be prepared to explain it — on all current issues or know how to get the correct response quickly.

All junior officers entering the Foreign Service go through basic training, called the A-100 course, before being assigned to their first post. They are introduced to the wide variety of issues they will face as representatives of their government abroad. One part of the training is a session on "answering tough questions," where each class member must stand before the group and face tough and sometimes adversarial questioning on a given topic. As we see from DeAngela's daily routine, that training is directly relevant to life as a diplomat. While the public affairs officers at embassies and consulates handle most of the press inquiries, all officers are expected to be able to present the views of their government at all times. And they do.

Junior officers serve in assignments that are no longer than two years, to ensure that they see different aspects of Foreign Service life before they are tenured as permanent officers. Officers are eligible for tenure after 36 months in the Service. Junior officers serve in positions in all sections of the embassy, but most serve in a consular position for at least one year.

"Being a junior officer is exciting and challenging," says DeAngela. "You begin to experience the fascinating cultures and places around you; you learn new languages; and you meet new people." The learning curve is extremely steep, as each job and each country of assignment is different and requires new skills. The cultural adjustment can be fairly dramatic. The junior officer is faced not only with getting established in a new country and culture, but also with adjusting to the culture of the Foreign Service and the requirements of being an official representative of the United States. This can be overwhelming as well as exhilarating.

At most embassies, the deputy chief of mission (DCM) serves as the mentor for junior officers, helping them navigate this new territory. In Pretoria, the junior officers have group sessions with the DCM to discuss career development. In China, where DeAngela served first, the DCM hosted a countrywide three-day conference for junior officers. The worldwide DCM mentoring program helps ensure that junior officers are not overlooked and have help establishing themselves in the Foreign Service.

Junior officers have the opportunity to make real contributions, and are treated as integral members of the mission team. In many countries, junior officers have a chance to work directly with the ambassador as a staff assistant. These jobs provide a unique oppor-

"Being a junior officer is exciting and challenging. You begin to experience the fascinating cultures and places around you."

tunity to be part of the highest-level happenings. Junior officers are often in a position to work on special projects that more senior-level officers are too busy to tackle. In Pretoria, DeAngela has been working on a project for the ambassador that aims to assess how the embassy can best support U.S. non-governmental organizations and foundations working in South Africa.

The U.S. is working toward a strong and lasting partnership with South Africa and is collaborating on health, education, peace and security, trade, and many other fronts. The U.S. mission to South Africa includes approximately 240 American personnel as well as over 400 South African nationals. DeAngela is one of eight officers in a 25-person public affairs section. No two days are alike in a public affairs section, and breaking news can turn a schedule upside down in an instant. Most mornings DeAngela looks through local papers and listens to radio and television reports to find stories of interest to the U.S. government. She is in constant communication with the media, writing press releases and arranging media briefings and responding to requests. She also writes speeches for the ambassador and the DCM.

DeAngela at a U.S.-South Africa high school video conference, speaking to South African students about differences between U.S. and South African pop culture.

A native of Kansas City, Missouri, DeAngela received a B.A. in international relations and African-American studies from Stanford University and a Masters of Public Affairs in international relations from the Woodrow Wilson School of Public and International Affairs at Princeton University. During her undergraduate studies, she was selected for a State Department Pickering Fellowship, which encourages talented minority students to consider the Foreign Service. Her experiences as a fellow "made an enormous difference and helped build a strong foundation that I have built my short career upon," she says. DeAngela is active in recruiting for the Foreign Service, and enjoys opportunities to introduce students to the Foreign Service.

She joined the Foreign Service in 1998, and spent the first year training in Washington, D.C. During training, she completed the A-100 course, the general services and consular courses, plus six months of Chinese language. She served one year in Guangzhou, China, as general services officer and then one year as a consular officer in Beijing, China. In between her China and South Africa assignments, she married her high-school sweetheart, Kelly J. Wallace, who accompanied her to Pretoria.

Foreign Service National
TAMARA BURKOVSKAYA
EMBASSY BISHKEK, KYRGYZSTAN

Foreign Service Nationals, the local employees working in U.S. embassies and consulates at every U.S. post in the world, provide the institutional memory for the missions. They remain at post as the American Foreign Service employees with whom they work move on to new assignments every two to four years. Known as FSNs, these employees staff just about every section of an embassy. They are drivers, electricians, interpreters, information technology professionals, political and economic assistants, switchboard operators, warehouse managers, customs expediters, security guards, and budget specialists, to name just a few. They provide American staff with background and context on local issues, contacts, and practices. They know the customs and traditions of the host country, and they help the embassy liaise with host country representatives inside and outside government. They keep the embassy running.

Tamara interprets for Senator Brownback and Kyrgyz President Askar Akayev.

Tamara Burkovskaya came to work at Embassy Bishkek in February 1992, one week after the embassy opened in the newly independent Kyrgyzstan, a former Soviet republic. At that time, the U.S. government faced the daunting task of opening missions in 14 new countries following the breakup of the Soviet Union in 1990-91. The embassy building was a small insecure structure in the center of Bishkek that had previously been an outpatient clinic. The building needed refurbishing, and Tamara played a key role in arranging licenses and permits with the local government, no easy task in a newly forming post-Soviet bureaucracy.

The first American employees were sent to Bishkek on temporary duty to help set up the embassy, find housing, and build a foundation for a positive U.S.-Kyrgyz relationship. Tamara was hired as an administrative assistant. She soon found herself involved in everything from negotiating with the new foreign affairs ministry on FSN contributions to the state-administered Social Fund to scouring Bishkek and its environs for a more suitable embassy building or plot of land on which to build an embassy. She was a vital member of the negotiating team that ultimately succeeded in leasing a sizable plot of land at the base of the Tien Shan mountains, now home to the chancery and ambassador's residence.

Tamara has seen Embassy Bishkek grow from a bare-bones outpost to its current lean, but respectable size. There are now 38 Americans assigned to the embassy in Kyrgyzstan and over 140 FSNs on its staff. After six years in the administrative section, Tamara moved to the political section, where she has worked as the senior political assistant for the past four years. The political assistant's job, in her words, is "to assist the ambassador, deputy chief of mission, and political officers keep abreast of all political, social, and economic developments in the country. This involves day-to-day, sometimes hour-by-hour, follow-up on various political events." Since gaining independence in 1991, Kyrgyzstan has been

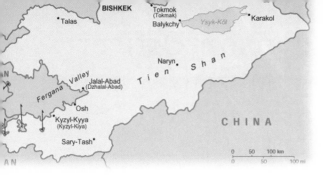

"Working at a
small post gives you
the luxury of wearing
several hats."

engaged in an ongoing process of attempting to establish a market economy and democratic institutions. This transition involves constant struggle, as people are torn between attempts to embark on a path of democratic development and temptations to fall back on old familiar Soviet ways of thinking. The embassy tries to play a positive role, whenever possible, in this transition.

To keep abreast of political and economic developments, Tamara follows mass media reporting, reviews government publications, and relies on her extensive contacts among government officials, human rights activists, non-governmental organization representatives, academics, and journalists. She conducts research on human rights cases and current legislative initiatives. She frequently accompanies the ambassador and other embassy officials to meetings with Kyrgyz government officials — including the president of Kyrgyzstan — and other embassy contacts, translating when necessary, taking notes, and contributing information as appropriate. Her primary responsibility as political assistant is to contribute to the embassy's reporting on a wide range of political and economic issues, but she notes that "working at a small post gives you the luxury of wearing several hats."

When a high-level visitor comes to a small post, just about every American employee and FSN must get involved to make it happen. Helping prepare for VIP visits by U.S. officials has been a significant part of Tamara's work at the embassy throughout her 10-year tenure. This "advance work" has included making appointments, arranging accommodations, compiling briefing materials, facilitating airport clearances, and liaising with the host government on numerous issues. After helping set up the visits, Tamara is often called upon to serve as interpreter for the visitors. She was the sole interpreter during negotiations for the Status of Forces Agreement that allowed for the deployment of U.S. troops at an air base near Bishkek. The air base supports U.S. and coalition military operations in Afghanistan; over 1,000 U.S. soldiers are currently stationed there.

Tamara with FSN colleagues at the Embassy Bishkek July 4th party.

Tamara is Russian, but has lived in Kyrgyzstan since the age of 10. She was born in the Altai region, now part of Russia. She has an M.A. in English from the Kyrgyz National University. She spent 12 years working at the Kyrgyz Research Institute of Cardiology, first as a translator of medical literature and later as head of the Medical Information Department. She has a 24-year-old son, Andrey, an interpreter. Tamara was the winner of the State Department's FSN of the Year Award in 1995.

Community Liaison Officer

LYNNE MURPHY AND JENNIFER WATSON

EMBASSY TOKYO, JAPAN

Jennifer (left) and Lynne.

The community liaison officer, better known as the CLO, is the point person for quality-of-life issues at an embassy. The CLO position is held by an embassy family member, not a direct-hire Foreign Service employee. The CLO plays a vital role in ensuring a healthy embassy community. Part of the administrative team, the CLO works with mission management and community members to maintain high morale through orientation programs, cultural and recreational activities, dissemination of information, and assistance with security education and family member employment. Top quality of life issues for most CLOs are schooling for children, employment for spouses and orientation for newcomers.

A good CLO serves as a critical link between embassy management and the greater embassy community, ensuring that lines of communication remain open and that management is always aware of the concerns of the community. Embassy Tokyo's co-CLOs Lynne Murphy and Jennifer Watson meet every week with post management to receive updates on developments and to relay current community concerns. These meetings became especially significant after September 11, Jennifer and Lynne explain, enabling them to keep abreast of security developments so they could help alleviate fear within the embassy community and the broader American community in Tokyo.

Lynne, 35, and Jennifer, 48, serve on the embassy's Emergency Action Committee, attending meetings and helping ensure that the community knows what it needs to know about emergency response planning. They helped update the earthquake handbook, including procedural guidelines for dealing with an earthquake or other natural disaster. "The expert consensus in Tokyo," Lynne says, "is that it is not a question of if an earthquake will hit but when." They developed a database of all American employees and family members, including information such as spouses' work contact information and children's school contact information, so the embassy can reach people if a crisis arises.

The embassy community served by Embassy Tokyo's co-CLOs is made up of about 573 American employees (from over 14 different government agencies) and family members, and about 375 Foreign Service Nationals. The CLOs also serve the five constituent posts in Naha, Osaka/Kobe, Nagoya, Sapporo, and Fukuoka, as well as the Regional Language School located in Yokohama.

Spouse employment is a major issue at all U.S. embassies today. CLOs help spouses become oriented to the local employment scene, and many CLO offices have job search resources, such as records of jobs held by family members in the past and contacts with local or international employers. In Japan, one long-term problem was the lack of an agree-

A good CLO serves as a critical link between embassy management and the greater embassy community.

ment allowing spouses at posts outside Tokyo to work outside the mission. Lynne and Jennifer pushed for change, which resulted in a successful agreement with the Japanese government to extend local employment privileges to these posts. "We will be able to attract many more qualified bidders for consulate positions as a result," said Embassy Tokyo's deputy chief of mission.

At every Foreign Service post, the issue of staff turnover presents a constant challenge. The CLO's role is to facilitate adjustment of employees and their family members to the host country and to embassy life. The easier the adjustment, the happier and more productive the whole mission will be. Being a large post, Embassy Tokyo has significant staff changes each summer, making welcoming and orientation a big part of the CLO's job in Tokyo.

Schooling is another priority issue for the Tokyo CLOs. No international school guarantees admission to embassy children, so the CLOs play an essential role in ensuring good access to good schools for embassy families. Lynne and Jennifer made significant progress improving the relationship between the embassy and the international schools, which had been eroding due to the inability of the U.S. government to compete with U.S. companies willing to pay large grants to schools to ensure access for their employees' children.

Leading the 2001 July 4th parade in Tokyo.

CLO activities vary somewhat by the time of year, with the fall devoted largely to welcoming and orienting newcomers, the winter months filled by correspondence with personnel bidding on the Japan posts, and spring and summer months busy with running the summer hire program and greeting newcomers as they arrive.

Jennifer was born in Nantucket, Massachusetts, but spent her childhood in Malaysia and the rural Philippines. She has a B.A. from the University of Pennsylvania with a major in Oriental studies. She married her FSO husband, Sam, during his first Foreign Service assignment, to Kuwait. They have also been posted to London, England; Washington, D.C. and Manila, Philippines, where she was also a CLO. They have two daughters.

Lynne had lived in seven states by the age of 20, "considering each home." She has worked as a photographer, a model, a bartender, and in retail sales and management, horse grooming, and child care. She married her FSO husband, Joe, after he returned from his first posting in the United Arab Emirates. She has accompanied him to Pretoria, South Africa, where she worked as the embassy newsletter editor, and Washington, D.C. Their next posting is to Apia, Samoa, where Joe will be deputy chief of mission.

Marine Security Guard
STAFF SERGEANT
TIMOTHY STEELE
EMBASSY YEREVAN, ARMENIA

Marine security guards stand watch over U.S. embassies and consulates around the world, always on alert for potential threats. Although the Marine security guard is not officially a member of the Foreign Service, one cannot paint a full picture of a U.S. embassy without mentioning the role of the Marines. The Marine guard is often the first point of contact for the visitor to an embassy or consulate, although some smaller U.S. embassies and consulates have local guard forces and no Marine security guard detachment.

The job of the Marine security guard is to protect people, classified information, and government property. Staff Sergeant Timothy Steele, 24, currently posted as a Marine security guard to Embassy Yerevan, says the Marines always keep in mind the acronym POPPER, which lists their key responsibilities: preserve order, protect property, and enforce regulations.

The Marine security guard detachment is still relatively new to Embassy Yerevan, a small embassy that was opened only 10 years ago when Armenia broke away from the Soviet Union and became an independent nation. Embassy Yerevan is affectionately known as "the little post that could," because of the generally upbeat morale and the ability to plug along without such amenities as regular electricity and water and reliable telephone communications.

Embassy Yerevan relied on a local guard force until a Marine security guard detachment was activated there in August 2001. Tim was assigned to Yerevan as assistant detachment commander. The Yerevan detachment was still being organized in December 2001, when the detachment commander, called the gunny (short for gunnery sergeant), had to depart on extended medical leave. Although younger than the other Marines in his detachment, Tim held the senior rank and so became the acting gunny until the arrival of the new gunny several months later.

There was still much organizational and administrative work to be done in setting up the new detachment in Yerevan. This was a challenging and rewarding time for Tim, who credits the other Marines for pitching in and offering their time to help.

A typical day begins before the sun comes up. He comes to post a half-hour early so he can prepare and "ease into the day." When it is time for his watch to begin, he relieves the Marine who was on duty all night at Post One (the main embassy entrance) and is "in the box" for the next eight hours. He monitors multiple cameras placed around the embassy. He controls entry and exit from the embassy building, and hands out visitor badges.

If there are protesters outside the embassy, he implements the notification system, with the dual purpose of alerting employees for security reasons and making sure the right embassy officer can determine the focus of the protest.

The job is not routine, Tim explains. "You never know what is going to come up. One day we're running drills, and the next day we could be monitoring a group of protesters marching in front of the embassy." Every day, the Marines inspect each embassy office to make sure employees are being vigilant about keeping classified documents secure.

When his shift ends at 2 p.m., Tim changes out of his official uniform and does a few hours of office work. Later he returns to the Marine House for exercise. He does volunteer work with local orphanages, coordinating Toys for Tots and Big Brother programs. Tim enjoys the outdoor cafes in summer and fall, and likes to watch people. He has little social contact with Armenians, spending most free time with other members of the American community. "There's not that much to do in Yerevan," Tim says, "We depend on one another for parties and games nights. We don't just work together, we play together. We really are a family here." Tim goes to sleep, or rather "hits the rack," between 9 and 10 p.m.

Tim appreciates the close-knit embassy community in Yerevan, preferring this environment to his last posting to New Delhi, where the American embassy community was much bigger. He says at a smaller post, "you feel more appreciated. In India, you're just standing there in a box. Here, people know who you are, they say hi, call you by name."

Tim at the firing range.

Tim grew up on a farm in Iowa, knowing from an early age that he wanted to join the military. His brother Shane was a Marine. Tim enlisted in the Marine Corps right after high school, attracted by the high profile and the opportunity to travel. In training, he learned of the importance of getting along with everyone in the embassy while still maintaining his security role. In a crisis, he has to be able to work with civilians, not only other Marines. Tim's first posting was to Camp Pendleton, California. He was then accepted into the Marine security guard program and sent to New Delhi, India, for two years. His next posting was to the U.S. Embassy Muscat, in Oman. During this tour he re-enlisted for an additional four years. In 2002 he was meritoriously promoted to his present rank of staff sergeant.

PART 2

A Day in the Life

One-Day Journals from
Embassy Staff around the World

From the political officer who rarely sees the light of day at NATO to the deputy chief of mission re-opening Embassy Kabul to the consular officer visiting an American in jail in Manila, these are the stories of everyday life in the Foreign Service.

In answer to the question "What is a typical day like in the Foreign Service?" most Foreign Service officers and specialists will say that there is no typical day. One of the most challenging, and rewarding, aspects of life in the Foreign Service is that the activities of the job are intimately connected to the situation on the ground in the host country. If you're the administrative officer and a coup occurs, your job can change in an instant from negotiating a building contract to implementing an evacuation plan. If you're the political officer, you'll cancel your meeting with parliamentarians to cover the demonstrations on the street.

Although day-to-day life in the Foreign Service is not predictable, it is possible to get a glimpse of the work of the Foreign Service during times of relative calm. We asked Foreign Service officers and specialists around the world to chronicle one day on the job. The selection of days will help illustrate the diversity of Foreign Service jobs and environments. Travel with USAID Mission Director Jonathan Addleton on a trip to the field in Mongolia. Spend a day on the road in Brazil with Under Secretary for Political Affairs Marc Grossman. Attend a Victory Day celebration in Vladivostok, Russia, with Consul General Jim Schumaker. Visit a tropical forest in Thailand with Regional Environmental Affairs Officer Ted Osius.

Share Consul General Eileen Malloy's workday in Sydney, which began early when her husband brought her the phone while she was in the shower. "An early-morning call from State's Operations Center is never a good thing," she says. She should know; she used to run the Ops Center, as it is known. The staff of this 24-hour nerve center for the State Department stands watch over world events, keeping the Secretary of State and others informed about significant events around the globe (political and economic developments, terrorist incidents, and natural disasters) as they occur. The Foreign Service staff of embassies and consulates serves as the critical link in this chain of information, and Foreign Service employees worldwide can pass information and be connected and informed through this network any time of the day or night.

A Political Officer at the U.S. Mission to NATO

BRUSSELS, BELGIUM

By Jim DeHart

| 8 a.m. | We stand on the street outside our house, my 6-year-old daughter and I, waiting for the school bus. It's our morning ritual — often the only time I see her each day.

| 8:20 a.m. | The car radio blasts French-language news, but I am too distracted by traffic to comprehend. Public transportation is not an option when you work at NATO headquarters, out near the airport. For the first time ever, we are a two-car family.

| 8:45 a.m. | The political section is quiet. I eat a croissant with my first cup of coffee as the computer fires up. Soon I have a cable on my screen — guidance for today's meeting with a delegation from Bulgaria, one of 10 nations eager to join the NATO alliance. The guidance looks familiar. It should be: last week we told Washington what it should say.

| 9:20 a.m. | I convert the cable into talking points for the ambassador — all about what Bulgaria must do to meet NATO standards, from fighting corruption to tightening export controls to downsizing its antiquated military machine. The reforms will be tough, but with memories of Soviet domination still fresh, NATO's defense guarantee is well worth the pain.

| 10 a.m. | I turn my attention to yesterday's unfinished cable on the ambassador's meeting with his counterpart from Uzbekistan, a front-line state in the war on terror. In 1994, NATO's Partnership for Peace expanded NATO's reach from Scandinavia to the Caucasus to Central Asia. Today, there are 45 ambassadors within three-wood range of the U.S. mission — and no shortage of meetings.

| 12 p.m. | E-mails and phone calls keep me from my cable. As thoughts turn to food, a document from NATO's International Staff pops onto the screen, proposing new tactics to support Ukraine's stability and democratic evolution. In two days, NATO members will meet to discuss strategy. If we want to lead that discussion — and we always do — we'll need instructions, and to get our instructions in time we'll need to propose talking points to Washington tonight. Incoming, outgoing, incoming: we're on an assembly line — only instead of slicing parts off chickens or fastening bolts on a Toyota, we're working with ideas, deleting and inserting pieces to build something called policy.

| 12:10 p.m. | I forgo lunch in the cafeteria to eat a sandwich at my desk. The paper on Ukraine is a painful read, nuanced beyond meaning and bleeding acronyms. It's the dialect of the international bureaucrat, something akin to English but far more wonkish and opaque: *In light of the NAC decision, modalities for stock-taking in the context of the Charter were agreed by the PC ...* Maybe this is the language I should have learned, French being all but useless here at NATO; only the Francophones care to keep it alive.

| 12:25 p.m. | I climb the stairs to the third floor to discuss the paper with my Defense Department colleague, then descend again to my office. After this burst of physical

activity, I go to work on a NATO-Ukraine guidance request, leaving aside my earlier cable.

| **2 p.m.** | The sun shines through my window, an event not taken lightly in Brussels. Somewhere out there, restaurants are serving duck and mussels and thick brown beer, or at least I think they are, based on some vague memory. This is the strangest part of NATO — the utter separation from the world outside. With all allies and partners on-campus, there is no reason to venture beyond the barbed-wire perimeter, no need to learn about Belgian society or politics or culture. To top it off, security arrangements in the mission preclude the hiring of local employees, normally the heart and soul of U.S. embassy operations. Without them, our isolation is complete.

| **3 p.m.** | My guidance request cable is done and out for clearance. Comments trickle in from colleagues, but most are too busy with their own cables to offer much. The Balkans, NATO-E.U. relations, missile defense: The volume of work is enormous and the issues complex, making us the masters of our portfolios. For those who want to do "policy," this seems the place to be. I read and answer a dozen e-mails.

| **4:55 p.m.** | I walk my revised cable to the front office, then chat with the ambassador on the way downstairs. In the conference room, the 19 permanent representatives of NATO (ambassadors from each NATO country) form a giant ring. To our right is the United Kingdom, then Turkey. Directly across from us, separated by the alphabet and yards of empty space, are the French. If only we sat next to them, close enough to swap jokes, maybe things would be different. There are no windows in the room, only ceiling lights in a funky drop-down design, circa 1971.

| **5:05 p.m.** | NATO's secretary general calls the meeting to order, then gives the floor to Bulgaria's foreign minister, who describes his government's plans for further reforms. The minister of defense speaks next. Afterward, the "permreps" take turns critiquing Bulgaria's efforts; their assessments are candid, sometimes brutal.

| **7:15 p.m.** | The meeting ends. The Bulgarians look tired but relieved; they have survived another test and understand better the work that lies ahead. Perhaps they take solace in being part of Eastern Europe's historic march toward democracy, human rights, and free markets — a transformation spurred by the lure of NATO and European Union membership.

| **7:30 p.m.** | Back in my office, I catch up on some reading and organize my papers for tomorrow. My guidance request on NATO-Ukraine is fully cleared, so I hit the send button and watch it drop from my queue. Unfortunately, my earlier cable on the Uzbek meeting is still there; and now I owe another cable on the Bulgarians, meaning that I have lost ground since showing up for work this morning.

| **8 p.m.** | I lock up my safe and head down the hall, with a quick good night to those still at their desks. The drive home is quick, the traffic thin as the sunlight fades. The Belgian houses are nice to look at, with their neat little gardens and winding stone steps. I wonder if I will ever be invited into one. But no, we are invisible to the locals, walking among them as if in a different dimension, a parallel world.

| **8:25 p.m.** | Dinner is waiting; a quick reheat in the microwave is all it takes.

As my wife puts our 2-year-old to sleep, I read about NATO in the *International Herald Tribune*. Yes, I think to myself, I worked on that issue, and that one too. At NATO, we are in the thick of it. Never before have I felt so plugged in — and so isolated.

A DAY IN THE LIFE OF...

The Deputy Chief of Mission
EMBASSY KABUL, AFGHANISTAN
By Ann Wright

| **4:30 a.m.** | My workday begins at U.S. Embassy Kabul. The 100-person Marine detachment is changing shifts, communications officers are pulling the cable traffic from Washington, mullahs are calling Afghans to morning prayer, and first light is peeking over snow-capped mountains surrounding Kabul valley. Colorfully-painted trucks, men in warm shawls on bicycles, boys pulling carts filled with everything from freshly-slaughtered sheep to window glass are passing by the embassy.

| **8 a.m.** | Three Marines march to the flagpole and raise the American flag. No matter how many mornings I see this ceremony in Kabul — ground zero for U.S. assistance to the Afghan people and potentially ground zero for al-Qaida retaliation for the war on terrorism — the daily raising and lowering of the flag are moving. I came in with the first diplomats in December 2001, and I've been here on and off since then. One hundred miles south of here, the largest coalition military action in Afghanistan, Operation Anaconda, rages as coalition and Afghan forces pound a large concentration of al-Qaida fighters.

| **8:30 a.m.** | The U.S. country team meets to coordinate U.S. government activities (except for military operations) in Afghanistan. Chargé d'Affaires Ryan Crocker chairs the meeting. Humanitarian and developmental projects for Afghanistan are the focus of today's meeting. Military, U.S. Agency for International Development, and administrative section representatives quickly agree on a plan of action for two infrastructure projects in Mazar-e-Sharif and Herat. Embassy political officers update us on regional political happenings. The defense attaché comments on local militia factions.

| **9:30 a.m.** | I'm off to a meeting at the Ministry of Foreign Affairs to go over a proposed schedule for an upcoming congressional delegation (CODEL) visit. We recently had CODELs on three consecutive days, and then on the fourth day Secretary of State Colin Powell arrived. The Afghan interim administration's tiny protocol office coordinates meetings with key Afghan officials for our delegations. With an ever-increasing number of diplomatic and international organization missions in Kabul, the protocol office must assist more and more official visitors. The protocol officers work nonstop, with few functional telephones, computers or fax machines to use.

We provide a proposed schedule of events and meetings, understanding that we will probably not get a response from the protocol office until the morning of the visit.

Congressional staffers will anxiously call numerous times to confirm the schedule, and we will reassure them that somehow the appointments will work out and the visit will be successful, but we can't say quite how — yet. This is Afghanistan, and things work in their own mysterious manner.

| **10:30 a.m.** | Back at the embassy, we learn that the long-awaited support flight will arrive on the same day as the congressional delegation. No point in trying to change the date; we desperately need the office equipment and construction materials on the flight. The contracted Antonov aircraft is huge and carries an incredible amount of equipment. Many trucks, our entire local staff, plus additional hired laborers will be needed to offload the equipment and transport it to the embassy. Wait, new information. We hear from the administrative officer that Washington is now sending two Antonovs. It seems impossible to handle both flights in one day, but fortunately, Kabul International Airport is open. The six bomb craters on the runway have been repaired, which saves us the 90-minute drive north to Bagram Air Base, a trip we had to make almost daily for the first 60 days we were here. Unloading two planes in one day will stretch our staff to the limit, but we need the equipment, so we'll manage somehow.

| **11 a.m.** | The building begins to tremble. Another earthquake. This is the third earthquake since we returned to Embassy Kabul. We stay put until the building settles down, then run outside to count heads and determine if there are any injuries. None reported. Next we survey the damage to the chancery. Several sandbags have fallen from the Marine lookouts on top of the embassy and one wall in a basement room has collapsed. The 35-year-old building is strong. The people in the Afghan villages to the north were not so lucky; reports come in during the afternoon of many deaths and thousands of houses demolished. For the next several days, USAID and the U.S. military will help the Afghan government and international organizations assess the damage and determine how the U.S. can help. We call the State Department Operations Center to let them know that we came through okay. They tell us the U.S. Geological Survey is reporting a 5.8-level earthquake with an epicenter about 100 miles northeast of Kabul.

| **12:30 p.m.** | Time for a quick lunch. We have no cooking facilities at the chancery, so a local Afghan restaurant prepares lunch for us daily. Mutton kebabs with rice, chicken with rice, dumplings with rice, and rice with rice are our daily fare. The meal is served from the embassy's bunker, which was built five years ago to provide protection for the Afghan staff during rocket attacks. It now houses the only flush-toilet and working shower on the embassy compound. Today, due to the earthquake, we don't tarry long in the bunker and take our lunches outside to eat at picnic tables.

| **12:45 p.m.** | Yells come from the bunker. The drain in our one bathroom has smelly, vile ooze coming from it. One of the local staff casually comments that perhaps it's time to pump out the septic tank. The 100 Marines and 20 Foreign Service staff who share the toilet agree. Replumbing the chancery building is the highest priority for our maintenance team. Old pipes that have not been used for 12 years are proving

hard to repair. Our heroes are the plumbers who deal daily with back-ups and blowouts of the most unimaginable mess!

| **2:30 p.m.** | We visit the United Nations mission to check on the status of delivery of office equipment, furniture and vehicles to the new government. The Taliban took everything they could transport, including the cash in the national treasury vault. When we leave the embassy, we do so in an armored car protected by the diplomatic security mobile security team. We pass through a meat market with sheep hanging from hooks and through a bicycle market where parts and tires are tacked to tree trucks and poles. We see big trucks bringing goods from Pakistan. Commercial life is returning to Kabul.

| **5 p.m.** | It's getting cold as the sun falls quickly. We return to the compound just in time for flag retreat. Then we head to the bunker for a bowl of hot vegetable soup from a huge caldron perched on a small stove in the narrow hallway. Soup and nan (flat bread) seem to satisfy most everyone at night. No one is gaining weight here, but no one complains of being hungry, either.

| **6:30 p.m.** | Washington is now awake, so it is time to call to report on the day's activities and write up reports on the earthquake and a proposed U.S. response. Some try to watch a little television, but we are still waiting for the satellite TV chip that will let us receive CNN and BBC via our satellite dish made from pounded soda cans. Until then, those who understand Arabic and Polish translate for the rest of us. Many read and chat with newfound friends for a while before heading off to sleep.

| **10:30 p.m.** | There's a flash-bang as a trip-wire on the compound wall explodes. We know to stay put until the Marine "react" team deploys to determine what triggered the explosion. Thirty minutes later they tell us another cat has snuck through the concertina wire and tripped the flash-bang. The cat was last seen high-tailing it across the compound.

| **11 p.m.** | Time to try to get back to sleep (hoping for no more earthquakes or flash-bangs tonight) and get ready for another busy day in Kabul.

A DAY IN THE LIFE OF ....

A Consular Officer
EMBASSY MANILA, PHILIPPINES
By Michael Newbill

| **7:25 a.m.** | I pull into the embassy compound, now torn asunder because of a comprehensive security upgrade in progress. I head for the American citizens services unit of the consular section, where I am serving as a junior officer vice consul on my first overseas assignment with the State Department. Our section serves one of the largest American expatriate communities in the world — 120,000 or so and counting.

| **7:35 a.m.** | I brew coffee and read e-mails. I reply to an American missionary cou-

Michael (right) and Foreign Service National Barry Bernardo inside Pasay City Jail in Manila.

ple living in the southern Philippines who inquire about the status of the immigrant visa petition for their adopted daughter.

| **8 a.m.** | The Filipina widow of a recently deceased American visits the embassy to report his death. She submits his passport and forms for the report of death. In the "Religion" category, the Philippine death certificate reads, "Believes in God."

| **8:30 a.m.** | Forty grumbling Americans apply for "Affidavits in Lieu of Legal Capacity to Marry," required by the Philippine government for all foreigners marrying in the Philippines. Since the U.S. maintains no central registry for births, deaths, and marriages, American applicants must execute an affidavit stating that there are no legal impediments to marriage. Marrying Americans is a big industry in the Philippines, and I notarize hundreds of affidavits each week.

| **9 a.m.** | A Philippine immigration official inquires whether a detained American has any pending drug cases against him in the U.S. The Drug Enforcement Administration office and the legal attaché at the embassy find pending state charges, but no federal charges.

| **9:25 a.m.** | I call to remind the American detainee that since he used another person's passport to enter the Philippines, we need proof of identity and citizenship from him before we can issue him a valid passport. His deep southern accent and methamphetamine-inflected cadence make him difficult to understand, but he agrees to have a former inmate, a Korean gadfly known in prison as "The Mayor," come to the embassy and submit the papers on his behalf.

| **9:35 a.m.** | I call the general services office to reserve rooms at the historic ambassador's residence in Baguio — the hill station established by the Americans at the turn of the century — for Memorial Day weekend. The cool climate of Baguio offers a refreshing break from the heat and pollution of Manila.

| **9:45 a.m.** | A consular assistant tells me an American and his Filipina wife, arrested the day before, are awaiting my visit. I receive a call from another American, whom we had helped receive treatment at a local mental institution. He says he is now doing fine and hopes to file a petition for his Filipina fiancée soon for immigration to the U.S.

| **10 a.m.** | I draft a cable about an American who was seriously injured in an explosion in the southern Philippines city of Davao. The previous Friday, a Foreign Service National and I visited the American in the hospital, reported his condition to his family in the U.S., and spoke to police and hospital officials. Over the weekend, we worked with his family and a medevac (medical evacuation) company to transfer him from Davao to Manila, where his burns could be better treated. The press reports that he is a known "treasure hunter" and that the police may file charges against him.

| **10:45 a.m.** | A friend calls to tell me that there is an electrical blackout affecting one-third of the country, including Manila. That explains the hum of the embassy generator in the distance.

| **11 a.m.** | Our senior passport FSN and I discuss issuing a transportation letter to the injured American so that he can be medevaced to a burn center in California on advice of his doctors in Manila.

| **12 p.m.** | Today we have pizza and pancit (a local noodle dish) for lunch to celebrate the fact that the entire staff of the American citizens services unit won awards at last week's embassy awards ceremony.

| **1:30 p.m.** | I visit the American citizen and his Filipina wife at the jail. Last year, the couple persuaded local police to arrest a suspect wanted on an outstanding warrant for the murder of their son. The suspect was later released, allegedly on the orders of a local congressman, and subsequently filed charges of "illegal detention" against the couple, prompting their arrest. I inquire about the charges, fill out an arrest report, and ask them to sign a privacy act waiver so I can discuss their case with relatives and other concerned parties. They attempt to persuade me to represent them in court; I persuade them to hire an attorney. I promise them that an embassy officer will attend their first hearing the following week.

| **3 p.m.** | While stuck in traffic, I try to catch up on the week's newspapers that I have brought along in anticipation of grueling midday traffic, compounded by the absence of working traffic lights because of the blackout.

| **3:30 p.m.** | I arrive at the hospital to check on the burn victim. The American insists that the explosion was no accident and that the U.S. government owes him a billion dollars for some prewar federal reserve notes he discovered. I suggest he ask Treasury for the billion dollars and convince him to let me take his picture for the transportation letter I will prepare for him.

| **5:30 p.m.** | I meet a Filipino friend to play squash at the Manila Polo Club. I lose.

A DAY IN THE LIFE OF...

The General Services Officer
EMBASSY YEREVAN, ARMENIA
By Kit Junge

| **3 a.m.** | I am up and getting ready to go to the airport to meet the diplomatic courier. Flights into Yerevan are always at "o-dark thirty," so we rotate duty as escorts for the classified pouch. Today it's my turn. I go to the airport and watch the pouches as they travel from the airplane … to the tarmac … to the transit area … to the truck … to the embassy … to the vault. Hypnotic. By the time I say good night to the pouches, it's time to come to the office for work!

| **7 a.m.** | I arrive two hours before the embassy officially opens to work through e-mails and meet with contractors and the maintenance staff, who all start early. I learn about electrical grounding, conduits, and plumbing during these early hours and suspect I will qualify as a mechanical engineer soon.

| 9 a.m. | The regular office staff begin arriving and the embassy opens for business. This is very early in the morning for Armenians. Never schedule a meeting outside the embassy before 10 a.m.! Over 15 minutes, I meet with the heads of each section in the general services office, including the motor pool and warehouse supervisors, the electrician, etc. My assistant gives me my schedule for the day and reminds me that I am invited to the ambassador's residence tonight for a reception focusing attention on the dangers of land mines in Armenia.

| 10 a.m. | The next few hours are a whirlwind of meetings, drive-by taskings, rounds to inspect works in progress, and planning sessions for the embassy space reallocation project. I meet with the project manager for the new embassy building to discuss start-up issues. Then I meet with the contracting officer for the Humanitarian Demining Center to establish procedures to comply with federal acquisition regulations.

| 12:30 p.m. | I drive out to a garage to inspect damage to our lightly armored vehicles caused by poor roads and decide how to repair them and prevent reoccurrence. Did I mention I am learning auto mechanics too?

| 2 p.m. | I rush back to show potential houses to members of the interagency housing board.

| 4 p.m. | I meet with two officers new to post. Then I return to my office to obligate U.S. government money for supplies, repairs and leases; authorize overtime; answer 28 questions on specific issues from staff; finish a presentation on the reallocation project for the ambassador; complete the sale of a vehicle for an employee who has left post; and negotiate the return of a property being dropped from the housing pool. At a small post like Yerevan, with only one GSO, there's no rest. Often there's not even time for lunch.

| 7:30 p.m. | I finally glance at a clock. Oh, no! I am late for the event at the ambassador's residence.

| 7:45 p.m. | Fortunately all of the important Armenian guests are late too, so I'm on time. The junior officer role at these functions is to mingle and protect: make sure all the guests are engaged and make sure the ambassador is free to talk and mingle.

| 9 p.m. | I head for home, which is a 10-minute drive from the ambassador's residence.

| 11 p.m. | The phone rings. It is the duty officer informing me of an emergency medevac being arranged for an embassy employee family member. My travel assistant has already arranged the tickets, but Yerevan's evacuation point is London. Because this family member is not a U.S. citizen, she has to have a visa to go there, but the only flight to London for the next three days leaves in six hours. Can I get a U.K. visa for her tonight, the duty officer asks? I put on my consular hat, and say I'll try.

| 3 a.m. | I leave the British Embassy with a visa for the embassy spouse. (Note to self: Remember to send a bottle of scotch to the British consul, who was asleep when I called her.) I go to the airport, where I started my day, to see the family off. In a few hours, I'll call Embassy London to make sure a medical officer from the embassy will meet the plane, find out where the husband will stay, arrange for flowers from our ambassador to be sent to the hospital room, and finally call the ambassador, the deputy chief of mission, the duty officer and the employee's section chief to inform them of the night's events.

The Consul General

CONSULATE GENERAL SYDNEY, AUSTRALIA

By Eileen Malloy

| **6:30 a.m.** | An early-morning call from the State Department Operations Center is never a good thing. My husband found me in the shower, thrust the phone into my hand, and said, "It's the Ops Center." He knew better than to hang around to ask what was up. The watch officer explained that our ambassador to an East European country had died and we needed to help the ambassador's daughter, a resident of Sydney, return to the United States for the funeral.

| **8 a.m.** | En route to my office, the security team hands me the card of an Australian who wants to borrow a U.S. flag for an upcoming exhibition match between the Sydney basketball team and the visiting University of Arizona team. I pass his request on to our wonderful general services office staff for action. My husband, our two daughters, and granddaughter are looking forward to attending that game, and now they will be able to take pride in our flag as well. I cannot join them; I'm speaking that evening at the American International School.

| **8:15 a.m.** | I ask our administrative officer to get his staff engaged in helping the daughter of the deceased U.S. ambassador clarify her transportation options. I also ask the consular officer to ascertain if the young lady's boyfriend can qualify for the visa waiver. By midday the admin section has arranged flight reservations and transport to the airport for the two of them.

| **8:45 a.m.** | The discussion at our staff meeting ranges from preparations for our July 4 reception and media issues of concern to the U.S. government to training for a new cable distribution system. The commercial officer stays behind to discuss a problem: U.S. firms might lose sales worth hundreds of millions of dollars because Australian companies are unhappy with U.S. restrictions on technology exports. It's not a new issue, but it is extremely serious for the companies involved. We review options.

| **9:30 a.m.** | I am off to New South Wales Premier Bob Carr's office with the public affairs officer for a briefing by high-school history teachers who have completed study tours in the U.S. Their study was supported by a grant from the Fulbright Fund to the premier. The topics range from the influence of rock music on politics to the U.S. labor movement. Since the teachers were in the U.S. on September 11, they agreed to include their impressions in a permanent archive. En route back to the consulate we discuss how to tie this in with a September 11 photo exhibition we are planning.

| **11 a.m.** | The consular chief tells me that the long-planned extradition of two drug dealers has been stalled due to a conflict between Australian laws prohibiting U.S. marshals from entering Australia with firearms and a U.S. law stipulating that U.S. marshals escorting prisoners must be armed. The extradition will eventually take

place, after things are sorted out with the help of our Department of Transportation officer.

| **1:30 p.m.** | I call the young lady who just lost her father and express my sympathy.

| **2 p.m.** | I draft an evaluation review statement for our commercial officer.

| **2:45 p.m.** | Finally I can get to the 30-plus e-mails that have arrived during the morning. In one e-mail, I brief the ambassador on a visit to Sydney by former National Security Advisor Sandy Berger, and in another I chat with a local Muslim contact.

| **3:40 p.m.** | I take a quick swing through the consulate to touch base with the consular and Air Force Post Office folks, but am careful to be back in my office in time for the ambassador's daily conference call from Canberra.

| **4 p.m.** | Our ambassador has instituted a daily conference call with the consuls general (in Sydney, Melbourne, and Perth) to brief us on his meetings and to let us, in turn, inform him about important visits and events in our districts. Today's call centers on how best to organize the four official July 4 receptions being held at our respective posts, and the results of the ambassador's consultations in Washington.

| **6 p.m.** | I head home for an evening with my family. Although I have an event to attend or host most evenings, Monday nights are slow and tonight I'm free. I've got one more stop first, to review representation events with our cook and clarify the guest lists and funding she needs. With that, another day of my three-year tour slips by.

A DAY IN THE LIFE OF...

An Information Management Specialist

EMBASSY HARARE, ZIMBABWE

By Kevin Rubesh

| **6 a.m.** | The alarm goes off for the first time.

| **6:15 a.m.** | OK … OK, I'm up.

| **6:45 a.m.** | I eat a healthy breakfast of Fruity Pebbles, straight from our latest NetGrocer shipment.

| **7:20 a.m.** | I arrive at the embassy. As I pause for the routine security check, I begin the morning greeting ritual with the local guards. "Mangwanani!" (Good morning.) "Mamukase?" (Did you sleep well?) "Dumuka kanamamukau!" (I slept well if you slept well!)

| **7:25 a.m.** | Depending on how many people have arrived at work before me, I have to dial, press, and swipe in as many as seven combinations and alarm codes to get to my office — the Information Processing Center (IPC) on the top floor of the chancery building. The Marine guard takes pity on me today and buzzes me through two of the doors.

| **7:30 a.m.** | The first job every morning is to open our communications circuits to

Washington and process messages that have been queuing up during the night. The department's official message traffic is all conducted using telegrams — a term that has been held over from the good old days of ticker tape. After processing the morning's message traffic and making sure it is all headed to the correct offices, it's time to do the daily backups on the various systems in the IPC.

Kevin in the "server room" of Embassy Harare.

| **9:15 a.m.** | I write a letter to our local telephone provider, TelOne, requesting the installation of a new leased line so that we can extend our network to the embassy warehouse on the other side of town. Once the line is installed — which can take anywhere from a week to a couple of months, depending on how many times a day we call TelOne — we'll have to test it to make sure the signal quality is good enough to handle our network traffic, and then install a new router and switch at the warehouse.

| **10 a.m.** | I wander down to the pouch vault to see what came in on this morning's courier-escorted classified pouch run. This morning's flight landed at 6 a.m., meaning that my partner-in-crime here at the IPC was up at 4:30 a.m. to get to the airport in time. I'll have the privilege of taking our courier and the outgoing pouch to the airport tonight. There is just one container today, bringing us long-awaited spare parts. I sign off on the receipt invoice and start closing up the outgoing pouch for tonight's run.

| **11 a.m.** | It's time to get back to work on our annual inventory of all of our IPC computer and radio equipment. After some digging in the files, we found out that this had not been done since 1994. That's a lot of catch-up work! We've been walking around the embassy for several days now with little yellow bar codes in our hands and glazed looks on our faces ... but we're almost done.

| **12:45 p.m.** | Where has the morning gone? Today I'm meeting a friend for lunch who is applying for a Foreign Service National computer position. Because most State Department tours of duty last from two to four years, often the real experience in our unclassified systems rests in the hands of our FSNs. We move on from post to post, but they stay behind and help the next batch of Foreign Service specialists settle into the job. We have a quick lunch at the embassy cafeteria, and I take him for a tour of the compound.

| **1:45 p.m.** | I meet the new assistant detachment commander for our Marine security guard unit. Every new arrival means that new computer accounts need to be set up. I create his classified and unclassified e-mail accounts, and then add him to the telegram processing system so that he can read the "cable traffic" from Marine headquarters.

| **2:20 p.m.** | Mail call! The unclassified pouch is in. These pouch runs come twice every week and bring everyone's personal mail. I help sort mail, then saunter off with my two boxes from NetGrocer and a stack of old bills. Ever since the anthrax threat cre-

ated the need to irradiate all our mail, mail gets to us "crispy" and three months late. The high temperatures melt credit cards and turn printed ink into glue.

| 3:30 p.m. | The budget office calls to tell us one of their phones is out. I replace the phone with one from our stock of spares.

| 4:45 p.m. | The ambassador's secretary calls. Someone pressed the send button on a telegram that should not have gone out. Is there any way I can get it back? I do a quick check and find out that yes, it has gone out, and unfortunately, no — once it's gone, there's no pulling it back.

| 5 p.m. | Most embassy staff head home. I have to meet our classified pouch courier at 6 p.m., so I decide to stick around and catch up on some overdue paperwork.

| 6 p.m. | I meet our truck driver and load the truck with the outgoing pouch, pick up our courier from his hotel, and drive out to the airport. The chartered DHL flight is scheduled to leave at 8 p.m. The plane doesn't land until 8:15 — not bad for Africa! By 8:45, after we spend 10 minutes trying to figure out how to secure the courier's seat to the floor of the plane, the flight is loaded up and on its way back to South Africa. We head back to the embassy.

| 9:15 p.m. | I park the truck at the embassy and drive home.

A DAY IN THE LIFE OF...

An Economic Officer at the U.S. Mission to the OECD

PARIS, FRANCE

By Brian McFeeters

| 8 a.m. | I walk with my daughters from our fourth-floor apartment near Place Victor Hugo to the nearby bus stop, where they and other children, many from the U.S. embassy community, catch the bus to the international school (American curriculum, with daily French lessons). Next, while my wife, Melanie, walks our son to a French pre-school, I set off on my bike for the 10-minute ride to OECD headquarters.

The Organization for Economic Cooperation and Development, founded in 1961 as an outgrowth of the Marshall Plan, is an economic policy organization with 30 member countries housed in Paris. Ambassador Jeanne Phillips leads the U.S. mission, a 40-person group made up primarily of State Department Foreign Service officers, with representation from Treasury, Commerce, Energy, EPA, and USDA.

I cover OECD committees in the areas of investment, taxes, financial markets, capital movements, and insurance, as well as a broad organizational reform project. The work involves extensive interaction with U.S. delegates from a spectrum of agencies, and with delegations from the other member countries.

| 9 a.m. | The workday starts with a quick hallway meeting with a Treasury tax official, Rocco Femia, who covers the OECD's Harmful Tax Project. He asks for help covering the two upcoming days of meetings on this project because the senior Treasury official who usually leads the delegation will be unable to attend. The project is aimed at promoting tax information exchange between OECD governments and a number of non-OECD jurisdictions named as tax havens in June 2000, as well as improving tax practices within the OECD. I offer to help as much as possible, which turns out to be not much.

| 10 a.m. | I attend the first 30 minutes of the Harmful Tax Project meeting, joining 80 other delegates squeezed into one of the smaller meeting rooms. The French co-chair of the group introduces agenda items in French. Many delegates tune in to the simultaneous English translation provided by interpreters overlooking the session from a glassed-in booth. After taking notes on the initial interventions from several delegates, I return to the office to prepare a briefing for Principal Deputy Assistant Secretary of State for European Affairs Charles Ries, who's visiting from Washington.

| 11 a.m. | I present a PowerPoint briefing to PDAS Ries on the status of reform, a project aimed at modernizing the way the OECD responds to members' priority issues. Ries, Ambassador Phillips, Deputy Chief of Mission Richard Behrend, and I discuss U.S. goals for the project and next steps.

| 12 p.m. | We all join DCM Behrend and other colleagues at his residence, near OECD headquarters, for a working lunch in honor of Ries with senior officials from the secretariat, who oversee its 1,600-person staff of economists and other social scientists. Discussion covers reform, the planned multiyear move of OECD headquarters while a main building is being renovated, and OECD's increasing menu of outreach work with non-member countries such as China, Russia, and various African countries.

| 2 p.m. | I finally have some office time to answer e-mails that arrived overnight, mostly from colleagues at the State Department. The OECD wants to co-sponsor a U.S.-China investment conference planned for the fall; I agree to look into possibilities, coordinating with Washington and Embassy Beijing. A senior OECD official is going to Washington, so I suggest a meeting at Treasury on corporate governance issues. The OECD Investment Committee is asking for members' views on what the priority projects should be for next year; I write up some suggestions and send them to Washington for approval.

| 3:30 p.m. | We hold a special mission team meeting with Ries. Officers give two-minute rundowns of their portfolios and hot issues under discussion at the OECD, including export credit guidelines and standard testing for chemicals under the OECD's environmental program. I talk about the ongoing Harmful Tax meetings. Ries explains the European Bureau's priorities and offers assistance to officers seeking onward assignments.

| 5 p.m. | I had planned to return to the Harmful Tax meetings, but am stopped by a call from Washington. U.S. government agencies have comments on the proposed U.S. government position toward OECD reform, to be discussed at an OECD ambassadors' meeting tomorrow. I spend the next hour and a half rewriting the ambassador's talking points for the meeting, then meet with the DCM, who suggests further adjustments.

| **7 p.m.** | I leave the office, later than usual. A nine-hour day is the normal schedule here.

| **7:30 p.m.** | After grabbing a quick dinner at home, I join Melanie and the kids for a playground session in the nearby Bois de Boulogne, a large forested park on the west side of Paris. School nights don't allow much time for enjoying the sights of Paris, but on weekends we often venture out to Loire Valley castles, museums such as Musee d'Orsay, and nearby villages such as St. Germain en Laye. After two years here, we've only scratched the surface.

A DAY IN THE LIFE OF ...

The Ambassador

EMBASSY VILNIUS, LITHUANIA

By John F. Tefft

| **6:30 a.m.** | My daily ritual begins when I take our 7-month-old wirehair fox terrier, Lui, out for his morning walk. I wish I had his energy! My morning cup of coffee in hand, I spend 45 minutes on the Internet, reading the *Washington Post* and *New York Times* (beginning with the baseball scores, of course).

| **8:30 a.m.** | A short drive to the embassy is followed by morning meetings with my office management specialist, Judy Thiessen, and my deputy chief of mission, Bill Davnie. We review the day ahead, making sure I have the necessary background material for my meetings, and go over scheduling plans for the following week. These days, Judy is hard at work with my spouse, Mariella, planning the Fourth of July reception, our largest representation event of the year.

| **9:15 a.m.** | Our Lithuanian press assistant, Andra Litevkaite, calls with a review of the previous evening's television coverage and a summary of the morning newspapers. We review several articles in the Lithuanian press. Then I turn to reading e-mails and telegrams that have come in overnight.

| **11:15 a.m.** | Jose-Angelo Oropeza, head of the Helsinki Regional Office of the International Office of Migration (IOM), pays a farewell call. We discuss two important areas of cooperation between the embassy and IOM: preventing the trafficking of Lithuanian women and helping the community of Visaginas adjust to the closure of the Ignalina Nuclear Power Plant. Both are difficult, long-term problems that we, along with the European Union, will have to address for many years to come. The European Union is requiring Lithuania to close the Chernobyl-style RBMK reactors as a pre-condition of membership in the union. The U.S. has made a major financial and technical contribution to improving safety at Ignalina.

| **12:15 p.m.** | I host a lunch at my residence — a home built by a Polish family in 1904 — for a group of experts on corruption in Lithuania, including academics, think-tank spe-

cialists and representatives of Transparency International. The corruption problem is a pernicious legacy from the period of Soviet occupation of Lithuania. U.S. officials regularly raise it as part of our dialogue on building civil society, and our assistance program funds several programs to improve ethics and to promote a better understanding of conflict of interest at all levels of government. This event is one of a series of issue-oriented lunches my staff and I are holding. They give us a chance to explore complex topics in a relaxed setting, where we can offer American hospitality and build our network of contacts.

| **3 p.m.** | Joe Bader, an energy security expert, pays a call. He is involved in organizing an upcoming NATO-sponsored conference on Lithuania's long-term energy security. Joe is very interested in having Lithuania purchase a modern, new reactor to replace the old Ignalina RBMK reactors.

| **4 p.m.** | I meet with my administrative staff to discuss our comprehensive embassy building and renovation program. Then I sign out several telegrams. Among them is a cable reporting on our implementation of recommendations from the inspection team that reviewed our work about six months ago.

| **5 p.m.** | I meet at my residence with Julijus Smulkstys, advisor to Lithuanian President Adamkus, on issues concerning the Holocaust and the Jewish community. We review a number of current problems, including the process for restoring the Vilnius Jewish Quarter and amending existing laws to provide for Jewish communal property restitution.

| **7 p.m.** | Mariella and I have dinner with former Minister of Culture Gintautas Kevicius and his wife, Ruta, at their home. Gintautas is a pianist and also the business agent for world-renowned cellist Mstislav Rostropovich, and has just been appointed director general of the Lithuanian Opera and Ballet with a mandate to inject new blood and ideas into the opera and ballet. It is an enjoyable dinner that provides a good chance to catch up on Lithuanian cultural affairs.

| **11 p.m.** | After watching CNN International News and looking over the *International Herald Tribune* and *Financial Times*, it is time for bed. But first, one more walk for Lui the wonder-dog.

A DAY IN THE LIFE OF...

The Regional Environmental Affairs Officer for Southeast Asia and the Pacific Region
EMBASSY BANGKOK, THAILAND
By Ted Osius

| **8 a.m.** | As car engines idle outside Ambassador Darryl Johnson's residence, his wife emerges, wearing a broad straw hat. "We're going to the jungle," Kathleen Johnson says, beaming.

Ambassador Darryl Johnson gives traditional Thai greeting to Khao Yai Conservation Project staff, May 1, 2002.

| **10 a.m.** | We are at the Khao Yai National Park Visitors' Center. I am biting my nails. Our well-rehearsed program should have started, but the media aren't here yet. Dozens of Royal Forest Department officials, forest rangers and non-governmental organization (NGO) representatives mill about, waiting for the program to begin. I am relieved to see that the ambassador and his wife, drinking coffee with our host, the top Forest Department officer, don't seem bothered by the delay.

| **10:30 a.m.** | Finally, an enormous double-decker bus pulls up. Four journalists climb out. Twenty were scheduled to come, but Bangkok is awash in rumors that today Burma's military junta will announce Aung San Suu Kyi's release. Five television stations and most print journalists have canceled our event to focus on the Nobel Prize winner in Rangoon. Two conservationists stop squabbling long enough to ask me who should speak first. Are my careful plans coming unglued?

| **12 p.m.** | We're back on track. Forty uniformed forest rangers demonstrate training drills: how to subdue a poacher, assist an injured comrade. Our Royal Forest Department host glows with pride. A controversial figure who frequently makes headlines in the local press, he designed the uniforms himself and brought discipline to a rag-tag crew of rangers. Three firefighters whiz down a rope from a hovering helicopter. Their team of 60 waves shovels, squirts at an imaginary fire, and sings in unison. One NGO trainer who frequents the park whispers, "I've never seen these people in the park before. Those shovels are newly painted. I don't think they've ever been used."

| **1:30 p.m.** | The ambassador announces grants to the Forest Department for environmental law enforcement. I wrote proposals four months ago, which Washington formally approved just days before this event. Sixteen embassies vied for funds, and we were awarded two-thirds of the grant money. I will make this program work if it kills me. Standing before a newly planted tree, the ambassador takes questions. Predictably, journalists ask about a debt-for-nature agreement scrapped by the Thai government. It's rubbing salt in a wound: I spent my first five months at post negotiating this deal, and groundless fears of biopiracy brought it down. The ambassador is a pro, fielding each question smoothly, yet I can't help imagining how sweet it would have been to sign that $9 million agreement here, surrounded by the trees we're trying to save.

| **3 p.m.** | It's raining heavily. Guards toting sawed-off HK-34s accompany us on our "quiet" hike through the forest. Our group of 40 probably won't be spotting any wildlife on this visit. Leeches crawl on my shoes. Still, the trees are majestic. Hundred-foot trunks loom like pillars in a cathedral. Roots are tangled into ghostly shapes. Thirty feet up, a ranger spots a hornbill nest. Jungle fowl cry out, and I can smell the bark of aloewood, pungent and exotic.

| **4:30 p.m.** | I'm no longer annoyed at the conservationist who has been delivering an

endless brief on wildlife protection as we trek through the jungle. After all, the ambassador has remained polite, unflagging, interested in each aspect of the program. We're treated to a rare sighting of Asian wild dogs stalking a small herd of deer. These dogs are fierce: a pack will chase a tiger off its kill.

| **5 p.m.** | The ambassador jokes in fluent Thai with kids at a youth conservation camp. He tosses out a soccer ball, stamped with the embassy seal. A former Peace Corps volunteer, he won't allow bad weather or scheduling delays to dampen his good cheer.

| **7 p.m.** | We dine on steak and fresh fruit under the stars, while a band plays "As Time Goes By." The lead singer wears camouflage pants: he is a ranger from the morning's demonstration. We're on the lawn of a house built 40 years ago by a Thai prime minister, General Sarit. Our host declares his preference for military governments, since they're "more efficient."

| **10:30 p.m.** | Our truck swerves to avoid a seven-foot python on the road. It slithers into the underbrush. We've seen deer, fisher cats and a few civets — weasel-shaped mammals with ringed tails — on our "night safari." A herd of nine elephants emerges from the dark to eat and frolic 20 paces from the road. "I never expected I'd live to see wild Asian elephants in the forest," Mrs. Johnson muses. All in all, a pretty good day in Thailand.

A DAY IN THE LIFE OF...
An Office Management Specialist
Embassy Abuja, Nigeria
By Llywelyn C. Graeme

| **7:20 a.m.** | I arrive in the front office, where I work as the office management specialist for the deputy chief of mission. I open the safe, turn off the hideous overhead fluorescents, and turn on the computers. Then I check my e-mails and print out the DCM's schedule for the ambassador. The ambassador, his office management specialist, and his staff assistant all go on leave tomorrow. The embassy will be closed for Eid-al-Maloud, the Prophet Mohammed's birthday.

| **7:30 a.m.** | I read all the cables addressed to the DCM and send notices to any sections that need to respond to urgent requests from Washington or other posts in the West Africa region. Then I watch a cleaning crew clean the front office. Personnel without top secret clearances are not allowed in secure areas of the embassy unescorted.

| **8:30 a.m.** | I prepare the cable and diplomatic notes announcing the ambassador's planned absence from post and noting that the DCM will become chargé d'affaires during the ambassador's absence. After the DCM approves the note, it goes to the Ministry of Foreign Affairs as well as to each of the 45 recognized diplomatic missions in Abuja.

| **9 a.m.** | Now that I've emptied the DCM's out-box, I fill up his in-box with new

Llywelyn

papers for the day. Then I set up five meetings for the DCM with various sections of the embassy.

| **10 a.m.** | I locate a phone number for the deputy national security advisor to the president of Nigeria, so we can schedule a demarche from the ambassador today. Then I attend a handover meeting with the ambassador's staff assistant and OMS to discuss issues that might come up during the ambassador's absence.

| **11 a.m.** | I design a newsletter to summarize local media reports for regular dissemination to the ambassador and the West Africa Bureau at the State Department. Then I design a form to electronically keep track of assignments the ambassador hands out at meetings. Somewhere in here I grab a Middle Eastern shawarma for lunch.

| **2 p.m.** | I send an emergency cable to the Office of Buildings Overseas that we thought we had sent three days ago. Then I stand watch over a plumber fixing a leaky faucet in the front office bathroom.

| **3 p.m.** | I prepare a diplomatic note about the increase in visa fees for Nigerians from 4,900 naira to 7,800 naira. Next, I receive diplomatic notes from the embassies of Eritrea, Saudi Arabia, Yugoslavia and the Papal Nuncio, and distribute and file them.

| **4 p.m.** | As the ambassador gets ready to depart, I make emergency copies of a set of drawings of the planned new embassy building for him to take back to Washington.

| **5 p.m.** | I track down the Lagos consul general, who's in Washington, so the DCM can speak with her.

| **5:30 p.m.** | I've read approximately 125 cables today. I search the State Department's "Intranet" for Web sites of Nigerian newspapers for the ambassador.

| **6 p.m.** | After sending an e-mail request to all agency and section heads for the administrative counselor, I call the Executive Secretariat of the Economic Community of West African States to ask if they have a copy of a communiqué on military cooperation among West African states. They do.

| **6:45 p.m.** | I fax the communiqué to the Bureau of West African Affairs before leaving the office to search for another shawarma for dinner.

A DAY IN THE LIFE OF...

An Economic Officer
Embassy Baghdad, Iraq
By Stephen Newhouse

| **5 a.m.** | I get the alarm clock off after the first ring. My roommate in the trailer sleeps through it, and I head off to the gym. In the morning twilight, it is warm, but still bearable, outside.

| **6:30 a.m.** | The huge marble palace ballroom cafeteria is just opening and there is already a line for breakfast, mostly GIs.

| **7:15 a.m.** | In the office, I run through my e-mail and news on the Internet. I prepare an agenda and talking points for today's meeting with the Minister of Planning and Development Cooperation.

| **8:45 a.m.** | I stop in to see the Ministry of Finance advisers before I head off to a staff meeting. We pause in mid-conversation when we hear a thud and the windows shaking. An explosion. My first thought is of the problems I will face if my trip out of the Green Zone is cancelled. My next thought is that it might not be such a bad thing.

| **9:30 a.m.** | I meet up with the Australian senior consultant to the Ministry of Planning. We don our body armor and meet his private security detail in the parking lot. We've got the standard PSD package: two fully-armored cars, four men with automatic rifles. We careen through the wild traffic of Baghdad, observing half-built and war-damaged buildings. We pass an incongruous new park, complete with a basketball court. The only thing missing is the kids.

| **10 a.m.** | We arrive at the ministry and head up to the minister's fifth-floor office, taking the stairs in case the power gets cut. He is pleased to see us, and we have a long talk.

| **12 p.m.** | We sit in on the inter-ministerial committee reviewing Iraqi agreements with donors on assistance issues. As they talk about power sector projects, I reflect on the amazing access we are afforded.

| **1:45 p.m.** | The meeting adjourns. There's lots more work to do, but the security detail has another trip scheduled for 2 p.m., so we need to leave. We are whisked back through the city.

| **2 p.m.** | Dropped back at the embassy parking lot, we head to one of the small restaurants springing up in the Green Zone. It is startlingly hot outside.

| **3 p.m.** | A colleague and I drive across the Green Zone to the Al-Rashid Hotel. We meet my contact outside the hotel, where he is patted down (again) and gets a visitor's badge. Inside, he shares his views about problems with the securities commission. We talk about his son, a university student, who was accidentally shot by the U.S. military. He convinced the soldiers to take the boy to the army hospital. His son should recuperate fully. He is philosophical: it was a mistake, mistakes happen, the soldiers apologized. I tell him how sorry I am.

| **5 p.m.** | Back at the office, I catch up on e-mail and then move on to writing the cable on my meetings. My colleagues and I compare notes on the day as we work. A car bomb at a local police station, 10 dead. An attack on a marine convoy. The Iraqi government allowed the newspaper linked to Muqtada al-Sadr to reopen.

| **6:45 p.m.** | I grab dinner in the cafeteria.

| **7:50 p.m.** | I arrive early, but a crowd is already gathered to hear Deputy Secretary Armitage speak at a town meeting by the palace pool.

| **8:15 p.m.** | I'm back in the office to finish my cable. I call the State Department and only when they fail to answer do I realize it is Sunday. The days really do run together here.

| **10 p.m.** | I finish the cable and send it to my boss for clearance.

| **11:30 p.m.** | A call from home: my 6-year-old tells me she has been hunting bugs. I am so tired, it's hard to focus on the bug story, but these calls do help bridge the distance between me and my family.

A DAY IN THE LIFE OF ...

The U.S. Agency for International Development Mission Director

EMBASSY ULAANBAATAR, MONGOLIA

By Jonathan Addleton

| **8:30 a.m.** | Our small delegation has breakfast at the Gobi Hotel in Moron, a small town located in the northernmost province of Mongolia, bordering Siberia. I'm with program manager and translator Mendsaihan (many Mongolians go by just one name) and driver Loya. The town consists of little more than a large collection of log cabins, resembling nothing so much as a desolate frontier town in Montana, circa 1900. We arrived yesterday in an aging Antonov 24 with bald tires and frayed seats. I sat next to a grizzled sheepherder who kept looking anxiously out the window at the rugged landscape below.

| **9 a.m.** | We visit the local power plant and see the five USAID-funded Caterpillar generators provided some four years ago. Nearby, a set of Russian and Czech generators from an earlier era languish, unused. Somehow, the chief engineer manages to keep the plant running.

| **10 a.m.** | Representatives from XasBank, a new USAID-funded micro-finance program that provides small loans to Mongolian entrepreneurs, meet with us. The bank is now expanding to cover all of Mongolia, a country larger than France, Britain, Italy and Germany combined — but with less than 1,000 miles of paved road.

| **10:30 a.m.** | We meet with a journalist working for *Rural Business News*, a USAID-funded monthly magazine with a circulation of 100,000, the largest in Mongolia. She mentions that she is working on an article about the economic impact of tourism on the Lake Hovsgol region.

| **11 a.m.** | We discuss the economic situation with the deputy governor of Hovsgol province. About the size of the state of Georgia, Hovsgol has a population of just over 100,000 — and *no* paved roads! Livestock — horses, sheep, goats, yaks, even a few camels — are the mainstay of the economy, though tourism offers some possibilities for the future.

| **11:30 a.m.** | We make a brief visit to the local Agricultural Bank offices, another rural financial institution that has been revived following the insertion of a USAID-funded management team. Although USAID has one of its smallest missions in Mongolia, the impact of our programs is significant.

| **12 p.m.** | Lunch at a local cafe located in a small log cabin in the middle of town con-

sists of "booz," the Mongolian national dish made of chopped mutton sprinkled with garlic and encased in dough.

| **1 p.m.** | We tour the local Buddhist monastery, nicely situated against a backdrop of snow-covered mountains. Despite strong efforts made to root out religion during Stalinist times, Buddhism is making something of a comeback in Mongolia. A half-dozen young monks dressed in orange robes chant out a blessing for our journey, one that will involve travel by Jeep across some 1,000 kilometers back to Ulaanbaatar, most of it on dirt track.

Jonathan outside a Mongolian ger (yurt) during a field trip to a rural area of the country.

| **2 p.m.** | We drive into the countryside to see a collection of ancient "deer stones." A few cows graze among the several "sacrifice mounds" as well as various standing stones, some with animals carved onto them. Some archeologists rate this site as the most impressive of its kind in all of Central Asia. The site figures prominently in a USAID-funded application to UNESCO to have the Hovsgol region declared a world heritage site, perhaps affording it eventual protection. We also visit a nearby river and an abandoned Soviet-era geology camp, quite large with its own well, generator and soccer field now covered in weeds.

| **7 p.m.** | Our Mongolian counterparts organize a dinner at the Gobi Hotel. Almost everyone at the table offers toasts to eternal friendship between the United States and Mongolia, though on this evening toasts are made with Scotch rather than the usual vodka. The chief engineer keeps referring to the importance of hydropower for Mongolia. For some reason almost every engineer in this country, on seeing a river, immediately wants to dam it.

| **10 p.m.** | I head off to bed while most of the Mongolian group retire for a round of billiards in the basement. The hotel room isn't much: the window is cracked, the curtains are torn, and the plumbing doesn't work. I pause briefly to watch the sun set over Moron. Tomorrow we will visit Lake Hovsgol National Park, another USAID-assisted program in Mongolia. The day after that, we begin the long journey back to Ulaanbaatar.

A DAY IN THE LIFE OF...

A Foreign Service Spouse

EMBASSY YEREVAN, ARMENIA

By Donna Scaramastra Gorman

| **7:30 a.m.** | Today's Saturday and it's our last week at post. I packed up my office at the embassy last week (I was one of the embassy's two community liaison officers). Four burly movers finished packing the contents of our house yesterday. Despite the

empty house, we're planning to have a party with some of our Armenian friends tomorrow. Today we're going shopping together, and afterwards they'll come over to help prep for the party. I'm making pizza tonight, but my cookbooks have all been packed, so I'm trying to remember the proportions for pizza dough. My son, Shay, sits in his booster seat, eating matzoun (Armenian yogurt) and laughing as I frantically search the kitchen for something to use as a pizza pan.

| **11 a.m.** | My husband, Bart, comes home from the embassy — he went in early this morning after receiving an emergency phone call. Shay stays behind to play with daddy, while I hop in a car with Armenian friends Murad, Mamikon, his wife Karine, and their son, Karen.

| **11:15 a.m.** | We're at GUM, the central produce market. My friends haggle with vendors over tomatoes, eggplants, and greens. They stop to translate for me every so often. As usual, all of the vendors want to know where I'm from.

| **12 p.m.** | We head outside to buy pork and chicken. We'll be making horovats — Armenian shish kebab. I'm always a bit uncomfortable at these outdoor meat markets, with their strung-up body parts and neatly stacked animal feet.

| **12:30 p.m.** | We're on our way again. But not for long. We make stops at the cheese store, the kitchen store, the soda kiosk, and a lemonade stand. All of this stopping and starting makes me miss those massive supermarkets in the States.

| **2 p.m.** | At the bakery, we order lavash (flat bread) at the window. Inside, women are rolling out the dough, wrapping it and lowering it into the tonir, an underground oven used for baking lavash. They let me photograph them, but wonder aloud why I want to do this.

| **2:30 p.m.** | We're home at last. Shay and Karen get acquainted.

| **3 p.m.** | We sit on the balcony, sipping coffee and preparing food for tomorrow. I start the pizza. Of course, the cheese grater is packed, too, so I slowly shred cheese with a butter knife.

| **4 p.m.** | Shay and Karen come upstairs to the balcony. They've been playing with the hose, and they're both soaking wet — the language barrier isn't a barrier for them.

| **5 p.m.** | The pizza is ready and we all dig in. For them, pizza is exotic — for us, it's just dinner. I look out at the mountain range that's been my view for so long: with a twinge, I realize that after this week I'll probably never see it again. I'll probably never see these people again, either. I get a bit choked up thinking about it.

| **6 p.m.** | Our friends leave, but they'll be back tomorrow for the actual party. Bart and I collapse on the couch, exhausted. Shay, however, is not exhausted. He wants to play — but with what? The TV is packed. The radio is packed. The books are packed. His toys are packed. So we head back into the yard, which is really mostly driveway, and run around until the sun goes down.

| **9 p.m.** | Shay's asleep. Bart and I sit down to read the post report on Almaty, Kazakhstan. It's hard to believe that in a few short weeks we'll be living there, in a country many Americans don't even know exists. I'll have a different view from my

window, and I'll have to start over making friends — but at least I'll (eventually!) have my cookbooks and my kitchen back.

| 12 a.m. | We stay up talking until midnight, speculating about how different our lives will be in just one month.

A DAY IN THE LIFE OF ...
The Human Resources Officer
EMBASSY SEOUL, KOREA
By Paul Gilmer

| 8 a.m. | Col. Bill Blocker picks me up from home in the 1995 Hyundai Avante I plan to buy from him. Since we, along with most of the embassy's other American employees, live on Yongsan Garrison, a U.S. Army post in the heart of Seoul, it is a short drive to the Army vehicle center where he can do the paperwork for the car. From there, we drive across the street to the embassy's general services compound to do the embassy-required paperwork.

| 9 a.m. | In my new car, I drive the 15 minutes to the embassy and attend the weekly administrative section meeting, chaired by my boss, Administrative Counselor Jim Forbes. I share results of the "Good Ideas Conference" that I attended in Hong Kong last week.

| 9:45 a.m. | I meet with Supervisory General Services Officer Jan Trickel to discuss the hiring of a desperately-needed engineer inspector and logistical arrangements for the afternoon's awards ceremony.

| 10 a.m. | An employee preparing to leave post in a month comes to see me. He has some human resources and grievance issues I am trying to help him resolve. Then I finish up a memo to junior officers soliciting candidates for the busy but rewarding ambassador's staff aide position. My secretary, Kim Moon Young, delivers the memo to Deputy Chief of Mission Evans Revere, who clears (approves) it within the hour.

| 11 a.m. | After I focus on recruitment of a cook for the DCM, I finally have time to access and print out the human resources cable traffic.

| 12 p.m. | I attend the monthly lunch for administrative and consular diplomats in Seoul. Although it is a no-host lunch, our office has made all the arrangements with the Seoul Club. About 25 attend, representing 20 different countries. I sit between colleagues from New Zealand and Switzerland.

| 2 p.m. | I chair a meeting of the Post Language Committee. Embassy Seoul is transitioning from five Korean-language teachers paid on an hourly basis to four salaried Foreign Service National teachers.

| 2:45 p.m. | I leave the language meeting before it's over in order to escort Ambassador Thomas Hubbard to the embassy's semiannual awards ceremony.

| 3 p.m. | The ceremony is held in one of the few venues we have available for large gatherings: the consular section waiting room. I am the emcee for the ceremony. About 190 people are receiving over 100 separate awards, but the ambassador is a real pro. We make it through in only 30 minutes, including "grip and grin" photos of winners with the ambassador and flower presentations. I even get to present the ambassador with his 35-year length of service award.

| 5 p.m. | I drive home in my "new" 1995 Hyundai with my daughter. She is home from college and has just finished her first day working as a summer hire in the consular section. It sounds like she had a good first day, even though I wasn't able to accompany her to work or have lunch with her.

A DAY IN THE LIFE OF...

A Public Affairs Officer

EMBASSY HELSINKI, FINLAND

By Crystal Meriwether

| 7 a.m. | I arrive at the embassy after a walk through the lovely streets of Helsinki from my home near the parliament building. The walk and the early start are the only ways to ensure some quiet time. I am a third-career "mature" junior officer in a two-American-officer public affairs section. I cover education and cultural activities. I am also the primary backup for the sole American officer in the consular section. No two days are ever the same.

| 7:30 a.m. | After I've made coffee, I go over the 60 e-mails waiting for responses: a seven-hour time difference with Washington and a hard-working, night-owl boss account for most of them.

| 8:30 a.m. | The consular chief is gone for the morning, so I open the section office. I meet with the six consular Foreign Service National staff members to discuss today's schedule.

| 9 a.m. | The public begins arriving at the consular section.

| 10 a.m. | Issues are developing that require special treatment: the call from the ambassador's office regarding a business visa request, the frantic woman awaiting papers to marry her U.S. fiancée who needs some hand-holding, and the serious medical evacuation case from Russia (Helsinki is the primary medevac site for Americans residing in Russia). The Foreign Service National consular staff provide quality service with smiles and the proverbial patience of Job.

| 11 a.m. | In between consular interviews, I meet with the State Department Educational and Cultural Affairs Fulbright officer who is visiting the embassy to evaluate our programs. We review her four-day schedule and make a few adjustments.

| 11:30 a.m. | Wearing my consular hat, I am too busy to complete my regular public affairs duties, so my boss represents me at a special meeting of the embassy committee that is planning an upcoming international women business leaders conference. She gives an update on the publicity subcommittee's activities arranging a digital video press conference. I provide the same stand-in service for her when she's unable to attend meetings.

| **12 p.m.** | I finish my consular duties and run upstairs to my regular office to check e-mail traffic while eating a yogurt and apple lunch. I type several replies, trying not to spill anything on the keyboard.

| **12:40 p.m.** | Donning my Fulbright Board Member hat (and only 10 minutes behind schedule), I'm off to the other side of the city for the board's quarterly meeting. Before we get to the formal business at 4 p.m., using expertise from my former life as a management consultant, I facilitate the annual updating of the three-year strategic plan for the Fulbright staff and board.

| **5:30 p.m.** | We wrap up the board meeting, and I catch a tram to my last event of the day. I am hosting a lecture at the League of Finnish-American Societies.

| **6 p.m.** | As assistant public affairs officer, I work on many cooperative ventures with the league, the largest U.S. friendship organization in the world. Tonight the league has invited our New York-Finland Police Fulbright exchange mid-career grantee to talk not only about the NYPD but issues of safety in New York City. Participants have many questions, and the interesting and lively discussion continues until 8:30 p.m. At the break, I thank our hosts and our guest speaker, and excuse myself.

| **9 p.m.** | Finally at home, it's time for dinner.

| **10:30 p.m.** | I take in the view from my window. Here in Helsinki, we are nearing Midsummer's Eve, when there are only four hours of darkness. The sky is still a robin's-egg blue.

A DAY IN THE LIFE OF ...

The Consul General

CONSULATE GENERAL VLADIVOSTOK, RUSSIA

By James Schumaker

| **7:40 a.m.** | The alarm goes off, and I'm out of bed like a shot. Tomorrow is Victory Day in Vladivostok, and there is a lot to do.

| **8 a.m.** | Over breakfast, I bring up a splitscreen of Vladivostok's 12 local TV stations on my laptop. Local TV news programs aren't very informative, but their pictures are, and I like to use them in my daily "E-grams," unclassified e-mails to the State Department.

| **8:40 a.m.** | Volodya, my driver, picks me up. Although Vladivostok is a low-terrorist-threat city, Volodya is very security-conscious, always finding new routes to get to the consulate. Today, we go over hill and dale and approach the consulate from a totally unexpected direction. Even the local guards are surprised.

James (right) with Pacific Fleet Commander Viktor Fyodorov.

| **9 a.m.** | I unpack my laptop. ConGen Vladivostok is an unclassified post, so all our reporting is unclassified and frequently done over the Internet.

| **9:15 a.m.** | My assistant, Lena, ducks her head in to give me a draft of the speech she wrote last night. I have been asked by Primorye Regional Governor Sergey Darkin to speak at the Victory Day ceremony tonight. I read the draft over quickly, practicing the tongue twisters Lena put in to test my Russian pronunciation. Clearly, I need more practice.

| **9:30 a.m.** | Vovka and Vika, my economic and political assistants, drop in to discuss the reporting tasks of the day.

| **10 a.m.** | I meet with a local academic, who is one of our best sources on political life in Vladivostok. It's really amazing how many people like to come to the consulate just to tell me stories. At other posts, you have to go to them. Here, everyone but the Navy and the Federal Security Service insists on coming to the consulate to meet. It saves me a lot of time.

| **11 a.m.** | Steve, our consular officer, stops by to discuss a sensitive visa case. Someone in the regional administration with possible organized crime connections has asked for a visa. Steve plans to temporarily refuse the application while referring the case to Washington for final guidance. His instincts are always sound in cases like this, and I agree with his decision.

| **12 p.m.** | I go upstairs to bum a soda from Andy, our administrative officer, and to discuss the events of the day. He says he has found a possible site for the new consulate office building. We agree to set up a time next week to take a more thorough look at it.

| **1 p.m.** | I start practicing my speech. The first couple of run-throughs are pretty rocky, but Lena helps smooth out the rough spots.

| **3 p.m.** | I finish the daily E-gram and send it out to my distribution list, which has grown to include virtually the entire national security side of the U.S. interagency community and many others as well. The Russian Far East is really the most interesting place imaginable.

| **4 p.m.** | Back to practicing the speech. After about the 15th run-through, I'm done, and go down to the administrative office, where Andy is throwing a small party for the local staff.

| **5 p.m.** | Volodya, Lena and I arrive at Gorky Theater and I greet my consular colleagues. Governor Darkin leads off with an excellent speech. He is followed by a "Hero of the Soviet Union" (war veteran), then Primorye Chief Federal Inspector Sergey Sherstyuk and Pacific Fleet Commander Viktor Fyodorov. I am fifth out of six speakers. Most of the 600 people in the audience are still a little suspicious of Americans, so I lead off with an extemporaneous congratulation to all the veterans who are in the audience. It goes over well. Then on to the speech, which is all about how the U.S. and Russia were

allies in World War II, and now we are once again allies in the war against terrorism. The applause is thunderous. Communist State Duma Deputy Svetlana Goryacheva follows me as the last speaker.

| **6 p.m.** | The speechifying is over, and the presidium is hustled off the stage and into the audience so the entertainment can begin. It is quite good this year, with talent triumphing for once over ideology. Patriotic songs, folk dancing, and circus acts are all part of the show.

| **8 p.m.** | With the performance over, 200 guests troop upstairs to the governor's reception. My consular colleagues congratulate me on the speech. I point out Lena as the real brains of the operation, and she turns beet-red.

| **8:30 p.m.** | The reception is in full swing. I haven't had anything to eat all day, so I proceed immediately to the nearest buffet table and start shoveling down caviar and blini. I have a good talk with the deputy Federal Security Service head for Primorye, who seems to have forgotten about the fact that I'm in the FSB's doghouse (last January, I covered a human rights demonstration in front of FSB headquarters). I also talk with Darkin's first deputy, Alexander Linetskiy, and after a vodka or two we attempt to sing a few bars of "Nam Zdes Zhit" ("We Are Meant to Live Here" —

Darkin's campaign song). This causes much merriment. I have a good chat with Governor Darkin and Admiral Fyodorov, who are both looking forward to the July 4 U.S. ship visit. An Aegis cruiser, the *USS Chancellorsville*, and a Marine landing ship, the *USS Fort McHenry*, will be coming to Vladivostok, and we plan to hold the July 4 reception on board the cruiser.

Victory Day on Vladivostok's Main Square.

| **9:30 p.m.** | The evening comes to a close. Tomorrow, although a holiday, will be just as busy, since the official military and civilian ceremonies will take place on Vladivostok's central square.

A DAY IN THE LIFE OF...

The Under Secretary for Political Affairs on the Road

BRASILIA, BRAZIL

By Marc Grossman

| **7:45 p.m.** | My special assistant, Mike Hammer, and I arrive in Brasilia and are met by embassy personnel. We proceed directly to the chargé d'affaires' residence for

an official dinner. Our embassy control officer, Dennis Hearne, uses the 20-minute car ride to brief us and go over the guest list. He also hands us a thick package containing cable traffic and other items sent from Washington. Before we arrive at the chargé's residence, Mike has gone through all the messages from Washington to determine whether any need immediate action.

| **8 p.m.** | Dinner guests include two Brazilian senators, the head of Brazil's space agency, a Supreme Court justice, and the head of the Central Bank. I make a presentation on our foreign policy, with a focus on Brazil, Argentina, and Colombia. Our dinner conversation underscores the breadth of our relationship with Brazil — in addition to our trade relationship, we have contacts ranging from education and environment to space research and health.

| **10:45 p.m.** | We head for the hotel. I check in, delighted that the embassy has set up Internet access in my room. Mike and I go over the schedule for the next day. I plan to wake up early to study for the under secretary-level talks, the reason for our visit to Brazil. The classified materials I will need tomorrow have been e-mailed from Washington through our secure system, so we did not have to take them on any airplanes. I ask that they be made available to me early the next morning.

| **6:30 a.m.** | Mike comes over with overnight cable traffic and we review the materials and issues for today's political consultations. Mike has gotten word that President Bush will be making a major announcement on steel and we make a note to check in with Washington about this before my press conference later in the day. We agree to meet again at 8 a.m. in the lobby. I study the materials.

| **8:25 a.m.** | We arrive at the embassy and proceed to a country team meeting where I'll seek advice on how to use my consultations to advance the mission's work. The country team briefs me on the issues the Brazilians are expected to raise; I am particularly interested in the military attaché's views on the possible U.S. sale of F-16 aircraft to Brazil, which I want to push. A key component of our responsibilities is to promote U.S. business. We review the expected steel announcement and I ask the public affairs office to work with the economic section to quickly compile statistics on U.S. steel trade with Brazil. Mike coordinates with the National Security Council and State's Bureau of Economic and Business Affairs.

| **9:15 a.m.** | I hold a town hall meeting with American and local embassy staff, stressing the need to live up to Secretary Colin Powell's high expectations of us. In the question-and-answer period, a Foreign Commercial Service officer asks whether other agencies are part of the secretary's vision or are just supposed to "eat popcorn in the stands." I answer that the secretary's vision is inclusive, that we need everyone to be advancing U.S. interests abroad, and that in his case, we expect him to be out selling the popcorn.

| **10 a.m.** | We arrive at the Brazilian Foreign Ministry and proceed to a conference room for the first session of talks with Under Secretary for Bilateral Political Affairs Gilberto Vergne Saboia. We review the political and economic situations in

our respective countries, talk about our bilateral relationship, including law enforcement and our military-to-military ties, and compare notes on situations in Argentina, Venezuela, Colombia, Cuba, and Peru. I urge greater cooperation, particularly in Colombia, where narco-terrorists threaten not only Colombia's democracy but the stability of the Andean region.

| **11:30 a.m.** | We proceed to our next meeting with Under Secretary General for Multilateral Affairs Luis Araujo Castro. We cover multilateral issues, including counter-terrorism cooperation, disarmament, the U.N., and the Organization of American States. I ask that Brazil vote for a resolution condemning Cuba's human rights record at the U.N. Human Rights Commission.

| **1 p.m.** | Ministry Secretary General Osmar Chohfi hosts a lunch for our delegation. The discussion focuses on the Middle East.

| **2:45 p.m.** | I ask the embassy press team what is in the news. Then I practice answers to what we expect to be the toughest questions. We check in with Washington, glad to hear the world is relatively quiet.

| **3 p.m.** | At the press conference, my opening statement highlights our strong relations with Brazil and advances our view that Colombia matters not only to the U.S., but to the hemisphere, and that Colombia's neighbors must do more to help defend Colombia's democracy. The questions are what we had anticipated: why doesn't the U.S. pay closer attention to Brazil, what are U.S. intentions in Colombia, and how does the president's steel announcement affect Brazil? I do my best. The press team's assessment is that it went well.

| **4 p.m.** | Our last appointment of the day is with National Security Advisor General Alberto Cardoso. We discuss improving our cooperation to fight drug trafficking. I note that the United States shares responsibility for the problem due to the demand for narcotics in the U.S., but stress that Brazil, working with its neighbors, should also work aggressively to stem supply. As I had done earlier at the Foreign Ministry, I pitch the U.S. F-16 sale.

| **5:15 p.m.** | We arrive back at the hotel with enough time to work out before departing for the airport. On the exercise bike I feel the intense humidity — a reminder that we are in the middle of the Amazon jungle. These trips are so packed that I don't get a chance to see much. I hope to return to Brazil — everyone raves about Rio and Sao Paulo.

| **6:45 p.m.** | We leave for the airport and in the van review with Dennis plans for reporting on the visit that we'd like to see from the embassy. Mike and I discuss follow-up actions, including thank-you letters to our hosts and embassy personnel who ensured the visit went smoothly, notes to assistant secretaries of various bureaus informing them of Brazilian positions on their issues, and a brief report for Secretary Powell. We arrive at the airport in time to pick up souvenirs for the office and kids. Mike picks up a gem: a Brazilian national soccer team jersey for his 6-year-old son.

| **7:40 p.m.** | The flight leaves on time. We will fly back to Sao Paulo, wait, trans-

fer to another plane bound for Miami, where we'll arrive at 5:30 a.m. (our second overnight flight of this trip), wait, then catch an onward flight to Reagan National at 7 a.m., arriving in D.C. around 9:45 a.m. tomorrow.

PART 3

The Foreign Service in Action

Tales from the Field

Foreign Service professionals work on the front lines of history. If something important happens in a country, the Foreign Service is there, keeping the U.S. government informed, protecting American interests and, where possible, playing a constructive role. Yet because the Foreign Service role in world affairs is often played behind the scenes, few know about the dangers faced and the skills and courage exhibited every day by Foreign Service employees serving overseas.

Andrew Young was the only diplomat who attended a court hearing for Aung San Suu Kyi's National League for Democracy parliamentarians in Rangoon, Burma, making sure the military regime knew America was watching. Overseeing the evacuation of American citizens from East Timor, Gary Gray and Victoria Alvarado faced rampaging militias and chaos during the aftermath of the East Timorese vote for independence in 1999. Tex Harris blew the whistle on the Argentine military during the "dirty war," meeting with family members of the "disappeared" and calling attention to the human rights violations taking place.

When Ambassador Chris Hill went into a refugee camp in Macedonia in the middle of the night, quelled a riot, and saved the lives of Roma refugees under attack, it was not covered on CNN. When Security Officer John Frese spent days rescuing Americans and others stranded in Monrovia, Liberia, during fighting between warring factions in a brutal civil war, no one made a movie.

Those who serve America in the Foreign Service do not do it for glory or for publicity. Yet recognition for the courage and the sacrifices made every day by the Foreign Service is warranted, and these stories give a glimpse of the ways that the Foreign Service makes a difference in the world.

One Riot, One Ambassador
MACEDONIA, 1999
By Charles A. Stonecipher

One summer midnight in the Balkans, an American ambassador walked into a refugee camp to try to quell a riot and save lives of Roma (gypsy) refugees under attack. He succeeded, and went home to bed. It wasn't diplomacy around big tables in grand rooms. The U.S. embassy had no responsibility to intervene, and few who were not there ever heard about it. But the actions of Ambassador Christopher Hill highlight the power of the individual Foreign Service officer's moral and physical courage.

At about 11 p.m. on June 5, 1999, my cell phone rang at home. It was Ed Joseph, an American working for Catholic Relief Services as a refugee camp manager at Stenkovac Camp, a few miles north of Skopje, the capital of the small ethnically-tense Balkan nation of Macedonia. Stenkovac housed tens of thousands of refugees from Kosovo, mostly ethnic Albanians. There was a riot going on, Ed told me, and it looked like people were going to get killed. A rumor had run through the camp that some Roma residents were Serb collaborators who had participated in a massacre of ethnic Albanians in Kosovo weeks earlier. A mob had formed in the camp to go after the two accused Roma families. The camp managers had just enough time to get to the scene, pull the Roma away, and get them inside the small building they used as an office. Two of the men had been very badly beaten and were only semi-conscious.

The building was surrounded by masses of angry people, pounding on the doors and barred windows trying to get at the Roma. If the mob got in, it was unlikely any of the Roma, including the children, would stand a chance. Ed was on the edge of the crowd by the front gate with other camp administrators, but their efforts to break up the crowd were not working. He did not know how long it would be before the mob would be able to smash its way into the building.

Ed knew that sending Macedonian police into the camp would only inflame the situation. We quickly ran through some ideas — NATO troops, Western European police officers from an OSCE training mission, a couple of others — but none had any prospect of working in time, if ever. The one trump card we could think of was the immense respect of the Kosovar Albanians for the United States, and for our ambassador in Skopje, Chris Hill, admired by Kosovar Albanians for his efforts to prevent the Kosovo conflict. Maybe he could calm the mob. It was a long shot, and we could not rule out the grim possibility that in the confusion Hill himself could be attacked or trampled. We could think of no other options, so I called Ambassador Hill.

Hill listened to my explanation of what was going on and our vague idea for his intervention, then simply said, "Yes, I want to get out there right away." Minutes later, Deputy Chief of Mission Paul Jones, Refugee Coordinator Ted Morse, Ambassador Hill, and I were standing at the gate to the camp, looking at the milling mass of people surrounding the building that held the Roma. We were met by Ed, an interpreter, and a gaggle of worried but seemingly powerless camp elders. As I listened to the din of noise from the unseen center of the crowd, the plan we'd concocted on the drive out began to seem a bit light.

We had decided to start with the interpreter using a bullhorn to announce that Ambassador Hill was coming into the camp to address the residents. The people closest to us would be able to hear it, and we'd wait for their reaction. Hill would then enter the camp flanked by Ted and Paul, holding lights. I would troop along with both arms overhead, displaying a towel-sized American flag I'd grabbed on the way out of my house. Between the flag and Hill's face we hoped to be allowed to pass far enough into the crowd for him to be able to make a speech at a spot where he could be seen and heard by as many people as possible. If he was able to calm things down, I'd try to get vehicles up to the building and we'd load the families and get out as fast as we could. There was no Plan B. Ambassador Hill looked around, said he was as ready as he was going to get, and headed for the gate.

Initially, our biggest problem was visibility, but the people on the edge of the crowd quickly turned to face us, recognized Ambassador Hill, and let us pass. With each step farther into the crowd, though, it got hotter, denser, and darker. Paul Jones grabbed a plastic crate for a podium as we pushed on. Around us the crowd swirled but people's attention increasingly turned to us. When we were about midway to the building, Hill stood on the crate while the interpreter continued announcing, "Ambassador Hill is here!" People yelled at each other in Albanian, "The Americans! Ambassador Hill!" Hill raised his arms for quiet and people began to shout, "Quiet! Everyone sit down!" Astoundingly, hundreds of men all around us began to sit on the ground so everyone could see and hear the ambassador.

Hill started to speak, and bit by bit, word by word, proceeded to transform the mob into an audience. He announced that NATO had just presented Milosevic with its non-negotiable plan to enter Kosovo. He told them how close Milosevic was to giving in, how close they were to being able to go back home. He said he knew they had suffered grievously and knew they thought the people in the building were guilty of atrocities, but they would bring no honor to themselves by taking matters into their own hands. "You know me," he said. "Give me the chance to take custody of these people and determine their guilt or innocence. I will do right by you. We have been through too much together to shame ourselves by making a horrible mistake." People listened, whispered among themselves. The whole crowd was now quiet, a mass of half-seen faces disappearing off into the darkness all around us.

As Hill spoke, I moved back toward the gate, using my awkward Albanian to ask people to clear a way for "the cars Ambassador Hill wants." This did not result in anyone actually moving — I was no Hill! — but at least they knew that vehicles were going to head that way. Two vans were waiting, and we inched them through the crowd and up to the building. The staff inside quickly loaded the battered Roma into the vans as hundreds of still-surly but now quiet men stood packed against the building, glaring. We drove out fast. I jumped out at the gate and the vans tore off for a hospital. Ambassador Hill was thanking the crowd and urging everyone to return to their tents. He was given a loud ovation and, amazingly, people started to drift off into the darkness. It was over.

Within a few days we confirmed from records that these particular Roma had all been in Macedonia during the time they were accused of having committed war crimes in Kosovo. Tension, rumor, and mass hysteria had created the mob that had come so close to killing them. Within weeks, Stenkovac Camp was virtually empty, its former residents back in Kosovo trying to pick up the pieces of their lives. The beaten men recovered, and those families, too, went their own ways.

We never talked much about that night again — each day at Embassy Skopje brought too many new problems and issues connected with the Kosovo crisis. But I've come to realize that night was characteristic of much of our work in the Foreign Service: We confront so many unknowns, we have so little time, and — on scales large and small — the consequences of our actions and inactions can be so extraordinarily profound.

Charles A. Stonecipher was the political officer in Skopje from 1998 to 2001. He joined the Foreign Service in 1989. Other postings have included Bissau, Guinea-Bissau; Calgary, Canada; Washington, D.C.; Tirana, Albania; and Geneva, Switzerland.

A Prayer for Democracy
BURMA, 1998
By Andrew R. Young

Down Rangoon's Merchant Street, past trees that offered scant protection to democracy activists shot by soldiers in 1988, I walk to the Supreme Court on a spring day 10 long years after those killings. Easy to find, the halls of justice are surrounded by troops and barbed wire. Burma's junta sealed off the court's front entrance, so now one enters via the back door — a fitting metaphor for a once-proud judicial system reduced to a mere adjunct of the military dictatorship.

A hundred National League for Democracy (NLD) supporters have gathered to support Nobel Laureate Aung San Suu Kyi's attempt to end the illegal detention of about 50 parliamentarians. Elected in the NLD's 1990 landslide victory, the political leaders have been harassed for most of the past decade. The regime has detained them for a year now without charge in the latest effort to break their spirit.

Faces of the Pa'o people from Shan State in central Burma.

These years have been rough on NLD supporters. Jailed in record numbers, they have lost jobs, family members, and seen a decade pass without freedom. Aung San Suu Kyi arrives to cheers of "Long Live the NLD!" She and the elderly party leaders (the younger leaders are in prison) know the outcome of the case in advance. Just as I do. Aung San Suu Kyi persists in a nonviolent struggle that inspires people to action, armed only with the conviction that they are right and protected only by party uniforms of homespun cloth.

Today's court date is a cynical ploy to suggest rule of law prevails. But no witnesses are allowed into the court. In fact, I'm the only diplomat who even tries to enter. Did the others give up? Or worse, have they begun to believe the lies put out by that classic oxymoron "military intelligence"? A Burmese bureaucrat backed by gun-toting soldiers tells me I must leave. My refusal is tolerated. In an attempt to reason with the junta, I explain on camera to the regime's videographer that this charade of judicial freedom is both obvious and pointless. Their attempt to force me to leave only ensures that I will stay. I wait.

When all seems quiet, I return to the embassy, after surreptitiously indicating to NLD supporters that the United States is watching, that they are not alone in their struggle for freedom. Within 15 minutes, riot police clear the street using truncheons. Such is the duality of a diplomat's power and impotence. I can prevent violence against democracy activists only as long as I can witness regime actions.

Weeks earlier a parliamentarian visited me. I suggested he not tarry, as covert operatives certainly saw him enter the embassy. He chastised me, saying, "I have a right to be here. A right to talk to anyone. I know what will happen to me. But before it does, I want to earn the trust of the people who elected me. I want to do something." Six months later, he was sentenced to 21 years in prison. He did nothing more than talk. But talk is dangerous in Burma. A monk once invited me into a monastery, through a locked door and down into a cave cut 35 feet into a granite hillside. At last he said, "Now, we can talk."

How courageous the Burmese are even when informants seem everywhere. I've met the bravest people in my life here. The Burmese struggle on for democracy despite the repression, despite setbacks. Here the State Department wages a righteous fight for justice. Some day, the Burmese people will win their freedom. I pray that change comes soon, comes peacefully, and comes before more lives are destroyed.

Andrew R. Young was a political officer in Rangoon from 1997 to 2000. In the Foreign Service since 1991, he has also served in Hong Kong, China; Washington, D.C.; Mumbai (Bombay), India; and Auckland, New Zealand.

A Coup
GUINEA-BISSAU, 1998
By Peggy Blackford

In June of 1998, I was looking forward to my imminent transfer back to the U.S. after three years as ambassador to Guinea-Bissau, one of the world's poorest nations. U.S. interests were modest in this former Portuguese colony. The small mission staff had two goals: to strengthen democratic institutions by providing training to the media and funding programs that empowered women, and to help create a more modern and stable economic development climate. One of our most successful programs was training Guineans in the simple technology required to process the cashew nuts that grew abundantly on trees all over town. Family income among some program participants had increased an astounding 700 percent. Peace Corps volunteers focused on agriculture and English-language teaching.

It was quiet in Bissau, perhaps too quiet. The president and his government were widely viewed by Guineans as ineffective and corrupt, albeit democratically elected. Change was inevitable, but neither diplomats nor Guineans were predicting immediate or violent change.

At 6 a.m. on Sunday, June 7, 1998, my doorbell began to ring incessantly. It was U.S. Agency for International Development Mission Director Nancy McKay, who reported that en route to her usual early-morning birdwatching, she had encountered armed men and heard automatic weapons fire.

The mission staff quickly assembled at the embassy. We learned that the chief of staff of the army, fired for his part in an arms smuggling scandal, had decided not to go quietly. Illiterate and unable to communicate in Guinea-Bissau's official language, Portuguese, he had been held under house arrest for some time and was little known to expatriates. Nevertheless, he was a hero of the bitter struggle that freed his country from Portugal and was revered by many in the military. They rallied to his support. The rebels quickly achieved control of two key military bases, one nearly adjacent to the embassy and blocking the only access to the airport.

An evacuation by air would be impossible. Office Management Specialist Diann Bimmerle, a veteran of several coups elsewhere, offered her experience and kept us connected to the State Department Operations Center in Washington. The U.S. military had no ships or aircraft close by.

Throughout the day, Vice Consul Bryan Hunt, a first-tour officer, fielded frantic inquiries from U.S. citizens and the press while at the same time tracking down all the Americans in the country, advising them to stay at home and in touch. Popular wisdom held that the coup attempt would blow over in a day or two. We had to question that assessment almost immediately when, early Monday morning, the shelling nearly blew us out of bed. Americans and others began seeking sanctuary in our residential compound across from the embassy.

Most people reached the embassy without incident, but two Peace Corps volunteers called desperately seeking our help. They were trapped in a hotly contested area of town. The local people were evacuating. Could we get them out? As I tried to decide whom to send on this dangerous mission, Nancy McKay spoke up. It was her neighborhood; she knew it well and would go. As the embassy vehicle pulled out of the compound, shelling began. The next hour, until everyone returned safely, was one of the longest of my life. Soon we were sheltering more than 50 people: Peace Corps volunteers, missionaries, businesspeople and tourists. We ransacked our homes for food, blankets, and towels, and prepared meals for our growing army of refugees. Peace Corps Medical Officer Karen Glucksberg treated an epidemic of stomach disorders and headaches brought on by nerves. Our newly-arrived summer intern, whose internship was to be short but memorable, spent hours destroying classified and sensitive documents. The staff moved mattresses to the embassy and we slept in our offices along with our eight cats.

The Portuguese Embassy informed us that a Portuguese freighter would take refugees to Dakar, Senegal. Space was available for our citizens. It seemed our best bet. On Wednesday, June 10, after a harrowing eight hours on the dock while shells went off around them, the vast majority of the Americans in Bissau, led by McKay and Peace Corps Country Director Brian Cavanagh, boarded the ship for a grueling but safe trip to Dakar. Those of us left in the capital drew a quick sigh of relief before setting to work to find evacuation routes for the 17 Peace Corps volunteers who lived outside the capital city. One by one we coordinated with authorities in Washington to extract them by air from tiny dirt airstrips or by roads heavily patrolled by the Senegalese and Guinean military. The last volunteer was airlifted out on Saturday, June 13. We gathered up the consular seals and took the cash from the safe. It was time for us to go as well.

Sunday morning, June 14, just one week after the coup began, we emerged from the embassy. The crumbling colonial town was deserted. Almost everyone had fled to the countryside, mostly on foot. Taking advantage of the mid-morning lull in the fighting, we drove to an isolated dock where we were picked up by a dinghy from a small tanker. Each of us boarded with a cat or two in one hand and a change of clothes in the other and set sail for Banjul, capital of neighboring Gambia. Twenty-four hours later, our adventure was over.

Meanwhile, back in Guinea-Bissau the war raged on for more than a month. Four of our homes were burned to the ground; the rest were looted. We lost almost all our prized possessions, yet we were the lucky ones. It took more than a year to broker a stable cease-fire, and for the Guineans it will be many more years before they truly recover.

Peggy Blackford served as ambassador to Guinea-Bissau from 1995 to 1998. She joined the Foreign Service in 1972 and also served in Nairobi, Kenya; Sao Paulo, Brazil; Harare, Zimbabwe; Paris, France; Bamako, Mali; and Washington, D.C. She retired in 2000 but continues to accept short assignments from the State Department's Bureau of African Affairs. She has taught at City University of New York and lectures on foreign affairs to various interested groups in the New York area.

A Taste of the Struggle
EAST TIMOR, 1999
By Gary Gray

From my first trips to East Timor in 1996 as a political officer in charge of regional affairs and the East Timor issue at Embassy Jakarta, I had witnessed the low-level insurgency under way since 1975, when Indonesia seized and occupied the former Portuguese colony.

Now, in the run-up to East Timor's crucial August 30, 1999, vote on independence versus continued integration with Indonesia, pro-integration "militias" had dramatically escalated their attacks. Even the most experienced East Timor hands questioned the wisdom of proceeding with the vote in such an unstable environment. Convincingly, though, my East Timorese contacts argued that while post-vote violence probably was inevitable, they could not afford to pass up what could turn out to be the only historical window of opportunity to achieve independence.

On voting day, fully 98.6 percent of registered voters braved intimidation to cast their ballots. Our hope that the presence of international VIPs, election observers, and foreign media would encourage restraint evaporated when pro-Jakarta militia elements fired shots and threw stones to force voters — and our own observer party, which included U.S. Ambassador to Indonesia Stapleton Roy — to flee from the Gleno voting station. In the next five days, as the nation-to-be was plunged into another episode of lawlessness and destruction, we got a taste of what the Timorese had faced for many years.

On September 2, the ambassador and his party departed and consular officer Victoria Alvarado arrived to oversee the evacuation of American citizens. By the next day the Timorese themselves began to take to the hills. On Saturday morning, September 4, UNAMET, the United Nations Assistance Mission in East Timor, announced the overwhelmingly pro-independence vote result at the Makhota Hotel. Hours later the hotel was set ablaze.

Dili was eerily quiet and deserted as Vicky and I, accompanied by Canadian diplomat Scott Gilmore, visited remaining concentrations of American and Canadian electoral observers, urging them to depart. At the local electric power office we found the last remaining Indonesian personnel packing up to leave — not a reassuring sight. Nearby, a few thousand people were in Bishop Belo's compound, a traditional safe haven, but just beyond the walls militia were shooting off rounds of automatic weapons fire.

Pro-integration militia preparing for an assault on a pro-independence neighborhood in Dili, August 1999.

At the chaotic police compound, where thousands of frightened Timorese were being loaded onto vehicles for transport to West Timor, I made an ultimately futile effort to convince the commander, a good contact and occasional tennis partner in more peaceful times, to provide protection to our citizens. By this time he had dropped any pretense of exercising real law enforcement authority. Passing a surrealistic scene of half-dressed Indonesian troops partying to loud rock music, we returned to our house and were startled by a long volley of automatic weapons fire unleashed by militia directly behind us.

During the seemingly endless, anxious night that followed we watched as half the sky was lit orange by the torching of an entire adjacent neighborhood. Word that an American member of the U.N. civilian police force had been shot and seriously wounded heightened concern that the situation was spiraling out of control. At around 3 a.m. the sound of motorcycles, voices, and then a few shots signaled the arrival of a group of militia at our house. They stayed outside for some 30 tense minutes, until, it seems, an East Timorese staffer of the Carter Center, a relative of one of the militia members, persuaded them to depart.

On Sunday, September 5, a typically beautiful Dili sunrise pierced the still rising smoke, and we cautiously ventured out. All seemed quiet, the perpetrators of the previous night's mayhem undoubtedly having retired into a drunken stupor. I gave our driver much of our remaining cash to fetch his family and flee. This left us with one car, thanks to the resourceful Gilmore, who had persuaded guards at the deserted New Zealand observer mission house to hand over keys to an abandoned Kiwi vehicle.

In early afternoon as we assisted more evacuees at the airport, Australian diplomats warned us that things were heating up again, and insisted we accompany them to their relatively protected consulate, the only diplomatic mission then in town. We had about five minutes to collect essential items from our house. I have a vivid memory of working frenetically to extract millions of Indonesian rupiah I had hidden behind a drawer.

Our respite at the Australian consulate proved short-lived. We heard via UNAMET radio that two members of the Carter Center staff, an American and a Canadian, had been apprehended by militia and detained. We first returned to the house to extract the other remaining Carter Center observer, under the noses of a truckload of armed militia parked nearby. At the police headquarters we found the other Carter Center staffers, arrested on charges of "reckless driving and assault." Two militia members on a motorcycle had pursued their car, attempting to fire at them, until they alertly turned into the motorcycle, forcing it off the road. With clear evidence to the contrary raging around us, the police insisted that Indonesia observed strict rule of law and that all legal processes must be completed. After much negotiation they agreed we could try to reach a settlement with the militia "victims." Luckily, the Carter staffers had ample cash, much of which then changed hands.

By now it was dark and our escorts had long since departed, but mercifully the drive to the airfield was short.

Portuguese journalists awaited a chartered aircraft there, with seats fortunately available for our Carter Center evacuees and for us as well. That refocused our minds on why we were in East Timor. Our "diplomatic presence" deterrence theory had long since lost validity. From

East Timorese children in their destroyed Dili neighborhood, October 1999.

our pinned-down position at the Australian consulate, our ability to report or influence events was limited. We had completed our duty to protect and assist American citizens, as all but a handful of die-hards had departed. Weighing the personal risks (including the immediate prospect of driving back to the consulate with no security escort along a dark militia-infested road), we decided it was a good time to leave.

The day after we departed, Bishop Belo's compound was attacked and his residence destroyed. Our house met the same fate. The Indonesian military and the militias carried out a wave of violence and destruction that reached virtually every corner of East Timor, ending only with the late-September deployment of a multi-national peacekeeping force.

I returned to East Timor several weeks later to find a scene of utter devastation. I will never forget the drive in from the airport, as our vehicle inched along through hundreds of bedraggled Timorese carrying a few meager possessions. Pillars of smoke still rose over Dili as the remaining Indonesian forces continued to torch their facilities. The East Timorese and the international community now faced the enormous task of reconstruction and institution-building, in many ways more complex and difficult than the process leading to the vote for independence. But at least the climate of fear had finally lifted.

William "Gary" Gray, a political officer in Jakarta from 1996 to 2000, was instrumental in establishing a full-time U.S. diplomatic presence in East Timor, which, after a three-year United Nations-sponsored transition, became the first nation of the new millennium on May 20, 2002. From July 2000 to August 2001, he served as principal officer at the U.S. Representative Office in Dili. Gary joined the Foreign Service in 1985, and also served in Bucharest, Romania; Pretoria, South Africa; Moscow, then-USSR; Washington, D.C.; Maputo, Mozambique and Kuala Lumpur, Malaysia. He retired from the Foreign Service in 2002 to become the chief of political affairs for the United Nations Mission in East Timor.

On Duty in Port-au-Prince
Haiti, 1997
By Robert A. Zimmerman

It began one Friday evening in July 1997. The Marine security guard on duty at the embassy radioed me about a frantic telephone call from an American citizen, who said that his daughter had been shot. According to the father, the girl had been taken to a Port-au-Prince hospital and had just six hours to live. I was the embassy duty officer for the week, so this case was my responsibility.

Fifteen minutes later, I arrived at Canape Vert Hospital and was met by two distraught parents and a crowd of about 30 onlookers. Fifteen-year-old Ornelia, the Haitian-American stepfather told me, had tried to commit suicide by shooting herself in the stomach. The attending surgeon said the wound destroyed about a third of her liver and she would die unless she could be treated right away in the United States. The girl's Haitian mother begged me to try anything to save her daughter.

My options were limited. There is no U.S. government fund to pay for medical evacuations of wounded Americans (or others) to the United States. Officially, all I could do was provide the victim with a one-page list of aircraft ambulance companies that offer medical evacuations.

The young victim had one other option: treatment at the U.S. military "fleet hospital" in Port-au-Prince. Located across town near the famous Cité Soleil slum and the airport, this MASH-like facility was built in 1994 to treat wounded soldiers who participated in the U.N.-sponsored military action against the government of General Raul Cedras. By now, the U.S. contingent was reduced to about 1,000 troops. American troop injuries were infrequent and the hospital concentrated on treating destitute Haitian nationals. Could they save this young girl?

Haiti's antiquated telephone system made calling the fleet hospital impossible. From the attending surgeon's office, I called the embassy and explained to the Marine Ornelia's condition and her prognosis. The Marine then telephoned the information to the U.S. military hospital, whose doctor-in-charge asked for even more specifics from our end. After about an hour, he agreed to admit the wounded teenager.

The ambulance ferrying Ornelia followed my car across Port-au-Prince at breakneck speed. Admission to the facility was closed to all but the victim's mother, stepfather, and the Haitian surgeon who accompanied her in the ambulance. The American physician determined that Ornelia's wounds were not self-inflicted, as her stepfather originally reported. The bullet wound trajectory in her stomach showed that she was shot from a distance. We would never know the real story.

After examining her, the military doctors told me that Ornelia would die in 24 hours if she were not evacuated to the United States. The hospital's chief asked me to help Ornelia's parents hire an air ambulance company and find a way to pay for the service. Out of the 12 air ambulance companies listed in our handout, only two answered the phone. Each was willing to fly to Port-au-Prince for about $50,000, to be paid up front. Ornelia's parents scraped together a few hundred dollars in cash and could charge up to $4,500 on their credit cards. Requests for help from relatives were fruitless.

The U.S. military then proposed another solution: locate a hospital in the States that would accept Ornelia free of charge. After many phone calls, a teaching hospital in Miami agreed to take her, provided that we could find transportation for her to the United States.

Commercial aviation was out of the question. Due to radar problems at the airport, planes could not land in Port-au-Prince after 5 p.m. However, at about 2:30 a.m., military personnel in Port-au-Prince contacted a Coast Guard pilot, who happened to be flying nearby. The pilot agreed to pick up Ornelia and take her to Miami.

Then the situation became even more complex. Ornelia was an American citizen and — even under those circumstances — needed a travel document in lieu of a passport to enable her to enter the U.S. I prepared this document. Her mother, who was not an American citizen, needed documentation from me in lieu of both a Haitian passport and a U.S. entry visa. The Coast Guard plane would not allow Ornelia's mother to fly with her and the stepfather did not plan to travel to the U.S. I had to then convince security personnel for a U.S. carrier that the airline would not be fined for allowing Ornelia's mother to arrive in Miami without the proper documentation.

A slew of telephone calls ensued. Working with U.S. military hospital personnel, I alerted the U.S. Immigration Service to expect two improperly documented entrants at different times. The Miami air tower was informed of the arrival of the Coast Guard plane. Security at Miami Airport was told to allow an ambulance to drive to the airport runway and take Ornelia to the hospital.

The Coast Guard flight carrying Ornelia left Port-au-Prince at about 6 a.m. As it took off, Ornelia's mother and stepfather lost the composure that they had maintained so well throughout the ordeal. I remained at the military hospital until about 10 a.m. to complete paperwork, thank the military hospital staff, and ensure that Ornelia's mother could board the Miami-bound flight that morning without difficulty.

Ornelia died in Miami two weeks later. I never heard from her parents again. Her death was never ruled a suicide and no suspects were ever charged with her shooting. The doctors and staff with whom I worked that evening were angry but powerless; we had to console ourselves with the knowledge that we gave her two extra weeks to live.

Robert Zimmerman was a vice consul in Port-au-Prince from 1996 to 1998. He joined the Foreign Service in 1993, and has also served in Paris, France; Yaounde, Cameroon; Buenos Aires, Argentina; and Washington, D.C.

Rescuing the Innocent
LIBERIA, 1996
By John Frese

Early Friday morning, April 6, 1996, fierce fighting erupted between several warring factions in Monrovia, Liberia, where I was serving as the embassy's regional security officer. The fighting soon engulfed the entire city and turned the country into a living nightmare for its inhabitants. No person or place, not even embassy personnel and property, was immune from the brutal fighting and wholesale looting that raged around the clock for weeks. Almost immediately, there was a complete breakdown of law and order, with thousands of undisciplined fighters roaming the city, killing, terrorizing, and looting. These fighters showed no remorse when killing innocent people and indiscriminately destroying whole sections of the city, including areas just outside the embassy compound. This was the most dangerous point in years of savage civil war that tore Liberia apart.

Since the fighting started with little warning, many people were caught off guard. At the embassy we began hearing of hundreds of American citizens and third-country nationals who were trapped in the city while fighting raged around them. Fighters were entering homes and threatening Americans with rape and murder. They were burning houses and businesses. The embassy started to receive pleas for help over the radio. We knew we had to do something. The ambassador turned to me and said, "Rescue them."

We decided to organize a small convoy of one regular and one armored vehicle (that's all we had) to go into the city and rescue those needing help. I drove one car; an embassy guard drove the other. Each morning, we traveled into some of the most contested areas searching for stranded Americans and third-country nationals. Before I left each morning, I would stare at a picture of my two children and wonder what they were doing. I missed them so much. Then, with constant gunfire and explosions in the background, I walked out to the convoy with an automatic weapon, a flak vest and a handgun. The other driver would give me a thumbs-up sign and off we would go in search of people. We spent entire days looking because we knew these people were relying on us to help them.

We couldn't travel anywhere in the city without witnessing the senseless destruction. The leaders of the warring factions had lost control of their fighters, many of whom were either intoxicated or on drugs. Each checkpoint manned by these fighters had a leader, some as young as 10 years old, who claimed to be a general. Each wielded machetes, knives or automatic weapons and thought he had absolute power over that particular area. We were constantly shot at and threatened. People often ask me what was going through my mind at this time. It was simple: I wished my car would go faster!

I was determined not to leave behind anybody who needed my help. The hugs and kisses from the families we brought to safety, and the expressions on their faces, made this effort worthwhile. At the end of the day, I would again look at the picture of my kids and doze off until another problem surfaced. Once daylight came, we were off again looking for more people. In all, we were able to rescue over 250 Americans, more than 100 citizens of other countries, and 40 United Nations officers.

At the same time, I was responsible for the protection of the growing numbers of people who took refuge in the embassy compound. It was especially tense during the first five days, before the U.S. military arrived, when I had to handle security incidents by myself. Fighters were constantly trying to force their way onto embassy property. Numerous times I had to leave the compound to try to reason with these fighters and defuse potentially deadly confrontations. Working with the local guards, Liberian National Police officers, and the five embassy Marine security guards, we established a defensive perimeter around the compound. At one point, I commandeered two West African Peacekeeping Force armored personnel carriers to dissuade approximately 30 heavily armed fighters from entering the compound. At the time, these fighters were pointing their weapons at our employees and threatening to kill them if they did not comply.

Foreigners were not the only victims caught in this war's crossfire. Driving around the city, I saw tens of thousands of desperate Liberians on the street. They, too, had been displaced by the fighting and needed food and medical attention. As soon as we knew all the Americans were safe, the embassy community turned its attention to helping the stranded Liberians. Another embassy officer and I procured several large trucks with local drivers and led a convoy to the seaport to obtain food and medicine. We then traveled through the war-torn city delivering these supplies to the people who needed them most. It was only after several aid organizations were able to travel safely within the city that we knew our work was done and we could go home.

Eventually we evacuated every American citizen who wanted to leave. We also helped citizens of other countries, whose embassies were unable to help them, return to safety. Throughout the ordeal, everyone in the embassy community came together. We were working for one goal and our success was truly a team effort. We were proud to be representing our country overseas. Every time I came back to the embassy compound after driving around the city all day, I would look up at the American flag and think about how lucky we were. I still have that flag.

John Frese was regional security officer in Monrovia, Liberia, from 1994 to 1996. He joined the Foreign Service in 1985 and has also served in Beirut, Lebanon; Guatemala City, Guatemala; Bamako, Mali; Kuwait, Kuwait; Lagos, Nigeria; Washington, D.C.; and Cairo, Egypt. John was awarded the Department of State's Medal of Valor for his leadership and courage during the Liberia crisis.

Fighting the 'Dirty War'
ARGENTINA, 1977
By F. A. "Tex" Harris

In October 1977, as a mid-level officer in Buenos Aires on my second overseas tour, I was asked by the embassy's political counselor to take responsibility for a new area of diplomatic activity — human rights reporting. I agreed, but had one condition: long-standing entry restrictions for uninvited visitors to the embassy had to be relaxed. I needed to be able to interview anyone who wanted to report the "disappearance" of a relative. The old embassy hands worried that this would draw a flood of relatives of victims, but I felt strongly that the job could not be done unless I could meet directly with the families of the "disappeared."

Within a few weeks, scores of people were flooding in daily to report their missing loved ones. The embassy, which had lived through months of terrorist threats and the terrible murder of a U.S. Information Service colleague at a branch post, had previously characterized the disappearances as part of a "dirty war" between left-wing terrorists and right-wing militias that continued after the Argentine military took power in a 1976 coup. My daily interviews told a different story. The hundreds of reports from family members demonstrated a massive, coherent, well-planned military effort to exterminate thousands of Argentine citizens who were targeted for their political beliefs, not their terrorist actions. I collected about two thousand personal accounts of disappearances on index cards. This was the raw data for my reporting to Washington.

At first, my cables to Washington detailing the human rights violations were applauded by the embassy staff from Ambassador Raul Castro on down. Then the consequences of the new Carter human rights policy became clear. U.S. policy towards Argentina changed. No longer were decisions being based primarily on the ambassador's recommendations, but also on the behavior of the Argentine government as documented in my human rights reporting. For the first time in American foreign policy, critical decisions were being based in substantial part on how a foreign government treated its own citizens. Argentina represented the cutting edge of a new dimension in American foreign policy — human rights.

A classic battle ensued, with the embassy front office trying to put a more favorable "spin" on my human rights reporting. As it became more difficult to report the full details of disappearances in diplomatic cables, I used airgrams, memoranda of conversations, and official-informal letters — none of which required front-office clearance — to send the facts to Washington by classified air pouch. My confrontation with senior embassy officials came to a head when one of my classified letters to Washington, which I had copied to the ambassador, was withdrawn from the diplomatic pouch. I was requested not to send it, but finally got the letter back into the pouch. The information in that letter resulted in the cancellation of a U.S. government loan guarantee worth several hundred million dollars for a major American corporation to provide turbine manufacturing technology to a front corporation owned by the Argentine Navy, which had been actively killing Argentine citizens. The embassy had not previously reported that key ownership connection to Washington.

As a young FSO, it was tough to fight with the ambassador. I stood firm on the need to get the full facts to Washington. I knew that my performance evaluation would suffer. I was almost fired for insubordination, but after an independent review, I was given only a formal warning. In 1993, with the benefit of 15 years of historical hindsight, the State Department awarded me its highest medal — the Distinguished Honor Award — for my reporting from Argentina.

Outside the embassy, things were easier for me. As an American diplomat, my information about the military junta's "disappearance" program authenticated the multitude of personal reports that journalists from around the world received when they came to Argentina. My Texas-sized (6'7") diplomatic presence and open support for the Mothers of the Plaza de Mayo, other human rights groups, and hundreds of families, showed that the American government and its people abhorred what was happening in Argentina.

At that time, I was focused on collecting and reporting the facts to the U.S. government. I also had the special responsibility to demonstrate the support of my nation to thousands of Argentines threatened by an outwardly sophisticated military junta gone out of control. Looking back on those challenging times, I know that one person can make a difference.

F. A. "Tex" Harris was a political officer in Buenos Aires, Argentina, from 1977 to 1979. He joined the Foreign Service in 1964, also serving in Caracas, Venezuela; Washington, D.C.; Durban, South Africa; and Melbourne, Australia. He was twice elected AFSA president, and held that office from 1993 to 1997. He retired in 1999 after 35 years of service. AFSA's Tex Harris Award for Dissent, given annually to a Foreign Service specialist, was established in 2000 in his honor.

After the Blast
KENYA AND TANZANIA, 1998
By Francis Njogu Mburu

On the morning of August 7, 1998, a truck entered the parking lot of the U.S. embassy in Nairobi, Kenya. Seconds later, the driver detonated a 2,000-pound bomb, injuring more than 5,000 people and killing more than 200, including 46

Njogu in his office.

at the embassy. Eleven Americans died. At almost exactly the same time in neighboring Tanzania, another terrorist bomb exploded at Embassy Dar es Salaam. More than 85 people were injured and 11 Tanzanians were killed.

I am Kenyan and I have worked for the U.S. embassy in Nairobi since 1982. I was at my job that Friday — the day now known simply as "blast night."

That day I went against tribal taboos by crying in front of my two daughters. That day, skin color and language mattered less. That day, the usually greedy men who operate "matatus" — our form of public transportation — let us ride for free. Even the rich man who usually drives alone in his spotless Mercedes Benz picked up three or four dusty, bleeding passengers and did not even care that his seats got stained.

For about five hours, the 42 tribes of Kenya were replaced with one big beautiful race of Kenyans. Foreigners became Kenyans too. Nationality didn't matter. Black looked white and white looked black. Nobody was an American, Italian or German. We all answered the call for help. This, I believe, is the way we were meant to be. I wish you could have witnessed the harmony and unification of mankind when help was in real need. On that day, in the midst of a horrendous event, I saw the true portrait of what God made us to be.

Working in the embassy's general services office, I had the chance to meet almost everybody in the U.S. embassy community. I delivered supplies to all the offices and furniture to embassy homes. I met new people every day and had many friends. I am sorry to say that on that day, my colleagues and I lost many good friends.

That day our work assignments changed. My colleagues and I were asked to watch over the place where we temporarily stored our dead co-workers. Family members of the victims came to identify their loved ones. It was our duty to help them. Their tears crushed us.

When I came home, my wife had to deal with a husband who had lost all hope. Even my old mama could not comprehend what had happened. After a long silence, she asked, "What have your bosses done to deserve this?" To my mama, in whose days young girls could not attend school, the only person strong enough to demolish the embassy was the ambassador. I explained to her what had happened and after understanding she just said, "The only thing you can do is to learn how to be strong and how to fly again when you are back on your feet, just like a lucky bird after a bad chase." Her words were encouraging and full of wisdom. She was right. We could do nothing but pick up the pieces and move on.

From the smoke of the flaming building, we came out hardened. In its ruins, we found love. From this horrible site, we learned to help others and to help ourselves. In the memorial park that now stands where the embassy once was, we remember the powers of respect that keep us unified.

May God bless Kenya. May God bless America. Together we remain.

Francis Njogu Mburu works in the general services office of the U.S. embassy in Nairobi, Kenya.

Assassination of an Ambassador
AFGHANISTAN, 1979
By Bruce K. Byers

Valentine's Day 1979 dawned clear and cold for members of U.S. Embassy Kabul. As we would soon see, it would be a day like no other in our careers. As press attaché at the U.S. embassy, I had worked with Public Affairs Counselor Roger Lydon and Ambassador Adolph "Spike" Dubs since my arrival in June 1978 to present official U.S. policy to the various ministries of the Marxist-led Afghan government and to help American journalists seeking access to Afghan officials.

Shortly after 8 a.m., Ambassador Dubs, a 56-year-old career FSO, was on his way to the embassy in his bulletproof vehicle when men dressed as Afghan police stopped it near the U.S. Information Service compound. Using a ruse, the armed men persuaded the driver to open his window, forced their way into the car and drove the ambassador to the Kabul Hotel in the city's center, where they took him hostage in an upper-floor room. The embassy driver returned to the embassy to announce the kidnapping. A stand-off ensued until shortly after noon. U.S. embassy officials believed they had persuaded Afghan Interior Ministry officials not to storm the room.

At approximately 12:30 p.m. a gunshot was heard from inside the hotel room. Immediately, police in the hotel corridor and on rooftops across the street unleashed a fusillade into the room that lasted more than a minute. Afterward, silence.

Moments later, Ambassador Dubs was found dead, his body riddled with bullets. None of us knew what this event meant or whether it was the beginning of a coup against the regime. President Mohammed Taraki and his pro-Moscow Marxist *Khalq* Party were in competition with the rival Marxist *Parcham* faction for control of the country.

Earlier that morning, when Lydon returned to USIS with news of the ambassador's kidnapping, I had decided to make an audio recording of embassy radio transmissions. I used a two-way radio tuned to the embassy's frequency to monitor and tape transmissions among colleagues at the Kabul Hotel and staff at the embassy and in vehicles moving between these locations and the Interior Ministry, where the Afghan government was trying to manage the crisis. Transmission quality varied, but afterward the tape helped embassy security officers construct a chronology of events for analysis in Washington.

In the hours and days that followed, I worked with Chargé d'Affaires Bruce Amstutz, Political Counselor Bruce Flatin, Lydon, and other embassy colleagues preparing responses to journalists from the United States, Europe, South Asia and elsewhere. Within 24 hours of the killing, dozens of Western journalists had poured into the city and wanted to know what impact the killing would have on U.S.-Afghan relations.

It would have been easy for us to hint at links between Soviet KGB and Afghan Interior Ministry officials, but we had to remain absolutely disciplined about information released to the media and the public. The truth was that we had few hard facts. Any public speculation by embassy officials could have precipitated more dangerous developments in a country whose government was already worried about its survival.

The circumstances surrounding the kidnapping and murder of Ambassador Dubs have remained a mystery. The three hostage-takers, who were taken alive by the Afghan Interior Ministry, were dead by the end of the day. They had been demanding the release of prisoners who the Minister of Interior claimed were not even in the country.

Through the traumatic days and weeks after the killing, the embassy staff and the international community pulled together. The chief responsibility of our embassy was to safeguard the lives of the more than 4,000 Americans living in the country and, especially, those in Kabul. We demonstrated that our mission would not be deterred from its responsibilities to represent our government and our nation in this geostrategically important country. In a simple ceremony in the embassy compound we honored our fallen ambassador, remembered as a U.S. Marine who had survived the bloody battles of the Pacific in World War II. We also went ahead with a community staging of *Oklahoma!* that buoyed everyone's spirits.

As in similar events in other U.S. diplomatic missions since — Khartoum, Beirut, Islamabad, Nairobi, and Dar es Salaam, to name a few — FSOs and their families stood firm in the face of terror and violence and represented the best ideals and values our country offers in the oft-dangerous field of international diplomacy. For those who served in Kabul, this was our tribute to "Spike" Dubs.

In December 1979 the Soviet Union invaded Afghanistan. During the 10-year-long Soviet occupation the U.S. embassy stayed open, supporting efforts to achieve a Soviet withdrawal. Ironically, the embassy was closed in 1989, following the Soviet withdrawal, and remained so for the next decade when domestic warfare among rival factions and the imposition of a ruthless regime under the Taliban and its allies in al-Qaida further devastated the Afghan people and destroyed vital social, political and economic institutions. Through all of this, Afghans have proven to be resilient, tough and freedom-loving.

The unprecedented September 11 attacks on America and the deaths of thousands of people from around the world triggered U.S. and allied actions that have led to the destruction of the Taliban and al-Qaida as political forces in Afghanistan. On January 17, 2002, Secretary of State Colin Powell officially reopened the U.S. embassy in Kabul and established diplomatic relations with the new Afghan government under Hamid Karzai.

If Ambassador Dubs were still with us, I believe he would applaud the return of United States diplomats to Afghanistan and American aid and support for the Afghan people. He would be proud to walk through the streets of Kabul once again and greet a free Afghan people.

Bruce K. Byers was press attaché at U.S. Embassy Kabul from 1978 to 1979. He joined the Foreign Service in 1971, and also served in Tehran, Iran; Bombay, India; Vienna, Austria; Bonn, Germany; Washington, D. C; Warsaw, Poland; and Manila, Philippines. He retired from the Foreign Service in 2000, and currently works part-time in the State Department's Bureau of Educational and Cultural Affairs.

A New Beginning in Kabul
AFGHANISTAN, 2002
By Suzann Reynolds

I was one of the first office management specialists sent to Kabul to help reopen the U.S. embassy in 2001. Just getting there was a huge challenge. From Tunis, I was faced with one of those "can't get there from here" scenarios. I flew to Geneva, and on to Zurich, where I spent the night. Then it was on to Karachi. I arrived in the evening and found a hotel for the night.

I returned to the airport early the next morning, only to be told my reservation to Islamabad had been cancelled. I managed to keep smiling as the manager ignored my plight and walked away. As soon as he was gone, the woman at the counter gave me a boarding pass and kindly waved me on. I was met in Islamabad by our "Kabul connection," with a red rose and a big smile (lamb to the slaughter?). The next morning I fought the airport crowd again, this time with 45 others destined for Kabul. We boarded the United Nations flight to Bagram Air Base, Afghanistan.

It seemed there was nothing at Bagram but the landing strip. The mountains of Afghanistan reminded me of Alaska's — rugged, jagged, snow-capped peaks. We were packed into a bus. The drive to Kabul took an hour, over bomb-damaged roads.

I arrived at the U.S. embassy at the same time as a new detachment of 89 Marines, and was shown my new

Street scene in Kabul.

home in the bunker next to the embassy. That's where I would room with seven other Americans for the next three weeks. Little did I know this would be a seven-day-a-week, 10-hours-per-day work schedule.

Over the next few days I was introduced to the conditions of the embassy, left vacant since 1989. Cars had been burned near the embassy front gate (now home to a machine gun emplacement) and a rocket had caused some damage to the embassy roof. However, most of the damage to the embassy was from neglect, not the Taliban. The lower floors were in terrible shape. We all worked in jeans. Each day, within a few hours of starting work, we were filthy from the mold, mildew, dust, and grime left from years of neglect.

There was no working plumbing in the embassy so the Marines, based on the lower floors, were using outdoor latrines. The underground bunker had the one and only bathroom, with shower. This bathroom was shared by the eight Americans living in the bunker and the 10 or so technicians who, having managed to clean up a few rooms, were sleeping in the embassy. The increasing number of congressional visitors added to our woes.

Most of the people who volunteered for duty in Afghanistan were long-time Foreign Service folks coming in for three to six weeks at a time. I was in awe of the high morale, how everyone tried so hard to accommodate each other (especially regarding the toilet schedule) and how everyone kept their sense of humor when it came to the tight living conditions. I told everyone the first guy to laugh at my yellow jammies with the baby chicks on them would be in serious trouble. One evening about 10 p.m., I left my bedroom, shared with two other women, to head to the bathroom. The new chargé, who had just arrived, was standing there waiting for the bathroom. All I could do was laugh and warn him not to make fun of the jammies!

Children of embassy Foreign Service National staff greet Secretary Colin Powell.

I hold vivid memories of my brief time at Embassy Kabul: sitting on the bed in our crowded little room trying to repair my woefully messed-up nails while Ann Wright laughed at my meager attempts to retain my femininity; watching the children of our Afghan workers wave little American flags by the embassy steps waiting for the arrival of Secretary of State Colin Powell; meeting a group of "survivors of September 11," who, having lost family during that tragedy in America, came to Afghanistan to help others and to heal their own wounds; being at a meeting in the conference room with 15 people hearing helicopters hovering overhead and not knowing whose they were; sitting in the sun during lunch outside the bunker and feeling an earthquake hit.

We all shared, unspoken, the knowledge that we were doing an important and dangerous job. It was an incredible feeling — being in the right place at the right time for the right reasons. Afghanistan has been center stage for our nation since September 11, 2001. I could relate to how New Yorkers must have felt cleaning up the wreckage in their city, showing the world these horrible acts of terrorism could never bring us down. The embassy was the "U.S. Liaison Office" when I arrived in Kabul. When Secretary of State Powell came to Kabul and elevated our status to "United States embassy" two days before I left, I was thrilled to shake his hand and proud of all we had accomplished.

Suzann Reynolds was an office management specialist in Kabul, Afghanistan, from December 2001 to January 2002. She joined the Foreign Service in 1992 and has served in Niamey, Niger; Beijing, China; NATO Brussels, Belgium; Riyadh, Saudi Arabia; and Port au Prince, Haiti. She is currently a rover, working at posts throughout the Middle East and South Asia.

Visiting the provincial airport in Jeremie, Haiti.

How to Save an Airport
HAITI, 1999
By Ken Merten

In any job, it takes courage to make unpopular decisions. In diplomacy, unpopular decisions can have international ramifications — and sometimes they can save lives. This is a lesson I learned when I worked in the economic section at the U.S. Embassy Port-au-Prince, Haiti.

Thousands of American citizens fly U.S. airlines into Haiti each week. In the late 1990s, the airport in Port-au-Prince was going through hard times. Underfunded for more than a decade, the airport had undergone several management changes. None of the airport officials knew who possessed airport or tarmac access passes. Any well-placed individual could obtain an airport pass to cut through the lines and red tape in this notoriously chaotic airport. Airport employees alleged that drugs and people were routinely smuggled through the lax controls and that several airport personnel were complicit. U.S. Federal Aviation Administration inspectors had been coming to Haiti monthly, repeatedly pointing out basic deficiencies. When a teenage boy was able to climb aboard a jet's wheel well and emerge three hours later in New York, U.S. airline officials began to realize that the lax security at the Haitian airport was a disaster waiting to happen.

The FAA wanted to take steps to sanction the airport, which was already at the lowest safety level ranking. The next level would be outright termination of flights to the U.S. However, political considerations in Washington — which had just helped return a democratically elected government to power — made it difficult to pressure the weak Haitian government. Policymakers felt that the Haitians would ultimately be unable to raise and subsequently maintain the standards at the airport.

My colleagues in the embassy's economic section had worked hard to develop a network of contacts in the Haitian aviation establishment. We knew there were competent, dedicated Haitian officials who could not only get the airport up to U.S. security standards but also maintain them. Working with visiting FAA representatives, U.S. airlines, and Haitian aviation officials, we crafted a strategy that would ultimately bring the airport up to U.S. requirements. The key, however, was to convince the Haitian government that it would have to take some radical steps or suffer severe consequences.

We advised our ambassador, Timothy Carney, that he should approach Haitian President Rene Preval and threaten suspension of direct flights to the U.S. if the Haitian government did not take appropriate steps. The suspension of flights would have cost the already weak government millions of dollars a month and generated tremendous ill will on the part of Haitian citizens. Moreover, it would have been a serious embarrassment to a country hoping to regain acceptance in the Hemisphere after years of unconstitutional government and international sanctions. The ambassador was skeptical that Washington would permit him to give an "ultimatum" to the Haitians, although he agreed it was the correct way to proceed.

In the end, Ambassador Carney followed the advice of his economic section and courageously made the unpopular decision to give the ultimatum. In his meeting with President Preval, Carney announced a fixed but reasonable date when the FAA would come to make a final inspection. Upon hearing about the ambassador's meeting, officials in Washington "gulped" but ultimately agreed that change was needed.

Security at the airport improved almost immediately. Within three months all the objectionable officials were removed, a procedures manual was created, and a strict ID system implemented. At the final inspection, FAA representatives pronounced the turnaround miraculous. Years later, the Port-au-Prince airport remains one of the most secure in the region and U.S. citizens and airlines continue to fly to and from Haiti without incident.

Ken Merten was chief of the economic section at U.S. Embassy Port-au-Prince from 1998 to 2000. He joined the Foreign Service in 1987 and has also served in Brussels, Belgium, at the U.S. Mission to the European Union; Bonn, Germany; Washington, D.C.; and Paris, France.

The Fall of Suharto
INDONESIA, 1998
By Shawn Dorman

By the spring of 1998, few Indonesians were holding on to the old Javanese belief that President Suharto — in power for over 30 years — had a "mandate from heaven" to rule Indonesia. Indonesia was on the edge of disaster. The Asian financial crisis had exposed the rot of corruption that was the underpinning of the Indonesian boom economy of the 1990s. Frustration with the repressive Suharto regime was reaching new heights. Students had joined forces around the nation to call for Suharto's resignation. Violent rioting and looting on May 14 — widely believed to have been sparked by forces in the military — left hundreds dead and parts of Jakarta gutted. Dangerous factions had evolved in the military, and no one was sure which way the military machine would turn: against the people, against the government, or against itself.

As the junior political officer at Embassy Jakarta, I had been working on the student and youth portfolio since my arrival in 1996. For several decades, the students had been quiet, forced by law to keep activities confined to campus and to limit political activity. I had already established good contacts within most of the key student and youth groups before many of them began publicly criticizing the government in 1997. Student leaders from radical Islamic as well as pro-democracy groups were always glad to meet, to help educate me on their vision for Indonesia. A number of prominent student and youth organizations formed an inter-religious coalition to push for "democrasi" and "reformasi" and began issuing public statements criticizing the Suharto regime. They kept me informed of their growing dissatisfaction, always appreciative of the attention from "the U.S. government." The political section sent frequent reports to Washington about the growing student movement.

By early May, student demonstrations had grown larger and the calls for Suharto to resign more explicit. Daily demonstrations numbered in the thousands of students, but they were mostly confined to the campuses, with the military guarding the gates outside to ensure they stayed put. Then the calls for Suharto's ouster grew louder, and demonstrations grew larger and began to move off campuses. When four students were shot and killed by snipers (almost certainly from the security forces) on campus at Trisakti University in Jakarta on May 13, the endgame began.

The embassy's emergency action team had been meeting frequently to plan what to do if the situation got out of hand. The situation did get out of hand on May 14, as riots erupted in many parts of Jakarta. The starting point was a demonstration at Trisakti University responding to the killings of the students. Security forces strangely disappeared just before mobs formed in many areas of the city, burning cars and stores, looting, and (we later learned) raping Chinese-Indonesian women. Chinatown was destroyed, as the long-pent-up resentment of local Chinese wealth was released. Hundreds of people died.

During this black day in Indonesia's history, every political officer was out on the street. Sometimes, the most that we can do is just be there, to bear witness.

We were in frequent contact with the Operations Center at the State Department, which by then had set up a 24-hour Indonesia Task Force. The May 14 riots were the catalyst that started the evacuation wheels at the embassy rolling. The following morning, an embassy-wide meeting was held to discuss the evacuation that would begin that night with planes flying into a military airport in Jakarta to carry out all family members and non-emergency employees, as well as any private Americans in Jakarta who wanted to go. I remained behind as my husband and 2-year-old son left home at midnight and, after a chaotic night at the airport, got on the 5 a.m. flight to Bangkok. Evacuees were greeted upon arrival in Bangkok and Singapore by the U.S. ambassadors in both countries, and embassy staff helped the exhausted evacuees with onward travel arrangements.

On May 18, students began to gather at the main parliament compound. Over the next two days, thousands came by bus from different universities and different cities, and now they were joined by their professors. They took over the compound, demanding that Suharto step down. The students were highly organized. They set up their own security system to detect provocateurs, those who might seek to turn the peaceful protest into something else. The military massed, heavily armed, outside the gates, but did not enter. The few of us still left in the political section — Political Counselor Ed McWilliams, Jim Seevers and I — took turns going to the compound, talking to students, gathering information.

The students were well-provisioned with food and water; clearly there were unseen supporters bankrolling this movement. As always in the land of the shadow puppet, there was much going on behind the scenes.

For days, there had been calls from many groups for "the people" to march to the presidential palace on May 20. The Indonesian government in Jakarta prepared for war with its own people. On May 20, the city was in total lockdown, an armed camp. Every street in central Jakarta was blocked by armed military personnel. There were tanks on street corners and barbed wire blocking intersections. I had slept at the home of the USAID mission director because everyone left at the embassy was living in consolidated housing for security. It was just as well: demonstrations had been blocking the only route home for several days. Because our vehicle had diplomatic plates, we were allowed through the roadblocks by the soldiers and went to work.

In the end, the Jakarta mass rally was called off — too dangerous — and thousands went instead to join those already encamped inside parliament. In other cities throughout Indonesia, thousands demonstrated. In Jogjakarta, the sultan led almost a million people in a street demonstration. To everyone's relief, the day was peaceful. But the message was clear: it was time for Suharto to go.

Suharto resigned the next morning, on May 21. That night, there was a festival atmosphere at the parliament compound. Even groups of soldiers broke into song and dance. The celebrating would end soon, however, as Indonesians would realize it is easier to tear something down than to build something new. The real work was just beginning in Indonesia's transformation to a democratic state.

Shawn Dorman was a political officer in Jakarta, Indonesia, from 1996 to 1998. Her other Foreign Service postings were to Bishkek, Kyrgyzstan, and the State Department Operations Center in Washington, D.C. She resigned from the Foreign Service in 2000 and now works for the Foreign Service Journal *at AFSA.*

Play Ball!
UKRAINE, 1991
By Carol Fajardo

My husband, Ed, and I were among the first Americans assigned to Kiev, then part of the USSR, to open a consulate. Soon after our arrival, the Soviet Union fell, Ukraine became an independent country, and our consulate became an embassy. I was our post's first administrative officer and Ed was the first consular official.

Everything was hard there: we had to book telephone calls in advance through the operator, our living room served as our office, and gasoline was scarce. Actually, almost everything was scarce. English was not widely spoken in Kiev, so our language skills improved quickly. As the administrative officer, my hands were full. There were always crises to solve and there never seemed to be enough resources to solve them.

Dima and members of the Little League team.

In this environment, it would have been enough just to struggle through the workday and collapse during our rare free time. But then we met Dima and Marina, a young Ukrainian couple who wanted to bring Little League baseball to Kiev. They found Ed, a baseball fanatic, and the rest is history.

We spent our weekends out at the "baseball field" that Dima had constructed out of scrap materials. There was no grass on the field — only dirt and stones. There was no way to level the field, which was usually covered in mud. A ragtag bunch of determined neighborhood kids showed up every day, practicing and playing with makeshift equipment. They had a rulebook that someone had laboriously translated word for word using an English-Russian dictionary. The words that did not translate well (ball, strike, base, out, foul) remained in English. Ed helped coach and I translated for him. There were a few other youth baseball teams, though they were not Little League, and our guys played them every chance they could.

We told our family back home what we were doing and suddenly we had castoff equipment from several Little League teams in California. All the kids received Point Loma (San Diego) pinstripe uniforms with caps. They were so proud of those uniforms. They laundered and pressed and mended them meticulously. Once they were in uniform, you could not distinguish them from Little Leaguers in the U.S. — except for the creases in their trousers.

They called themselves "Almaz." It was the perfect name. Almaz is the Russian word for a diamond in the rough. The play on "baseball diamonds" was lost on many Ukrainians, most of whom were unfamiliar with baseball, but it was the right name all the same. These young men were all Almaz.

The team was rather down one day. There was to be a baseball tournament in Crimea, a region in Ukraine along the Black Sea, and there was no way they would be able to raise the funds to travel there. We asked how much they needed. It turned out that, due to the collapse of the local currency, they needed just under $200 for the whole team to go. Ed and I decided we had found a very good use for some of the hardship pay we were receiving. The press of embassy

Dima (left) gives the team trophy to Ed and Carol to present to the Point Loma team.

business prevented us from attending, but every one of the kids went. I don't know if they won the tournament or not — the outcome didn't seem nearly as important as their participation.

While sitting with those kids on the bleachers, watching the balls take crazy hops off that horrible playing field, I think we did almost as much to advance U.S. national interests as we did in our day jobs. The Almaz players will grow up cherishing our national pastime and, I hope, understanding that Americans don't all look and act like the ones on TV. I have to admit, though, that isn't the reason we did it. We made some good friends and we had some fun.

I can still hear Dima at the start of each game in his heavy accent calling out, "Play ball!"

Carol Fajardo was administrative officer in Kiev, Ukraine, from 1991 to 1992. She joined the Foreign Service in 1985 and has also served in Sofia, Bulgaria; Nassau, The Bahamas; Colombo, Sri Lanka; Seoul, Korea; Frankfurt, Germany; and Washington, D.C. She does not play baseball.

Calling All Ambassadors
IRAQ, 2003
By David Dunford

Four days before the beginning of our second war with Iraq on March 19, 2003, the State Department asked me to go to Iraq as a senior ministerial adviser. I had retired from the Foreign Service years earlier, was not looking for work, and was in fact giving talks in southern Arizona sharply questioning our Iraq policy. I did some serious soul-searching about whether I wanted to be part of an operation that I had predicted would go badly. My wife and son persuaded me that, regardless of what I thought about the wisdom of the war in Iraq, the debate was over and it was now important to my children and grandchildren that Iraq reconstruction go well.

After three weeks of bureaucratic wrangling between the State Department and the Pentagon about who was to get various jobs, I was assigned as the senior coalition representative to the Iraqi Foreign Ministry. I flew to Kuwait on April 11, 2003, where we waited until U.S. Central Command judged the environment in Baghdad "permissive." On April 24, I flew with several other "shadow ministers" to Baghdad on a C-130 transport plane. We were delayed several hours at the Kuwait military airport when a U.S. general's plane broke and he took ours. We couldn't help but wonder what priority the U.S. military was giving our mission.

When I signed on, I understood that my job would be to go to the Foreign Ministry, take the elevator up to the minister's office, find out who was in charge and take it from there. The reality was very different. Daily life in Baghdad combined elements of a backpacking trip and prison camp. It took three days in Baghdad to link up with military civil affairs officers who could physically get my team to the ministry. We found the main building systematically burned and looted by departing Saddam loyalists. They had stripped the outbuildings of all windows, furniture, and electrical and plumbing fixtures. Windblown documents served as ground cover. An affable young Iraqi materialized out of the rubble and identified himself as Hamid from Protocol. Hamid agreed to get word to as many ministry employees as possible and we would all meet back at the ministry in two days. Soon after he departed, I had second thoughts. Had I set up an ambush? But two days later 150 employees were milling around as I arrived. We selected the nucleus of a small steering group to run the ministry.

Gaining control of Iraq's 69 diplomatic posts abroad was my highest priority. High-ranking Ba'thists and Iraqi intelligence operatives stationed abroad still controlled significant resources. I worked with the steering group on a simple message calling on heads of diplomatic missions to cease representing Iraq, to secure all files, passports, and money, and to return to Baghdad within 30 days. Our biggest challenge was how to get this message to Iraqi diplomats abroad given the almost complete lack of communications inside postwar Iraq. A young employee typed the message in Arabic on his laptop, we rescued some usable ministry stationary from the rubble, and we printed the message at Baghdad's version of Kinko's. We brought the message, typed and signed by the steering group's senior Iraqi, back to the palace to the only working scanner in Iraq. We then e-mailed the scanned message to the Iraqi embassies in Amman and Damascus and they, in turn, forwarded it to other Iraqi posts around the world. We then set up a Hotmail account that became the main channel for communicating between the ministry and Iraqi posts abroad.

The most fascinating part of this assignment was the chance to meet and interact with people I would never have otherwise encountered. In early May 2003, I met with the Iraqi who had been acting deputy foreign minister when the war began to give him the message that he was fired. I read in his eyes as we parted, "If our roles were reversed I would crush you like a bug." One day in early June, I interviewed in rapid succession the returning Iraqi ambassadors from Tripoli, Tehran and Damascus. All were surprisingly eager to cooperate even though they knew they would not keep their jobs. In fact, three-quarters of the Iraqi ambassadors elected to return, a much higher percentage than we had anticipated. The others, with one or two exceptions, quietly disappeared.

Throughout this adventure I was blessed with superb assistance from retired FSO Allen Kepchar, Lt. Colonel Alex Sonski, Ambassador Radu Onofrei from Romania, and Jacqueline Lawson-Smith from the British Foreign Office. However, the real credit for our success must go to our Iraqi colleagues, individuals of great skill and character. Two in particular, Akila al-Hashemi and Bassam Kubba, remain engraved forever in my memory. Akila accepted an appointment as the first woman on the Ministry Steering Group in early May, and ably led an Iraqi delegation to a U.N. donors meeting in New York. In July, she was one of three women appointed to the Iraqi Governing Council. In September 2003, assassins took her life. Bassam was serving as deputy foreign minister when he was gunned down in June 2004. While mourning their loss, I remain hopeful that Iraqi leaders like them will make it possible for Iraq to emerge from the nightmare of Saddam's rule to become a viable state.

David Dunford served in Iraq from April to June 2003. He joined the Foreign Service in 1966 and retired in 1995, having served in Quito, Ecuador; Helsinki, Finland; Washington, D.C.; Cairo, Egypt; Riyadh, Saudi Arabia; and Muscat, Oman, where he was ambassador. He currently teaches at the University of Arizona and does consulting.

Stuck in Ayana
ETHIOPIA, 1992
By Robert C. DeWitt

The spring of 1992 was an unstable time in Ethiopia. The country's ruling coalition, the Ethiopian People's Revolutionary Democratic Front (EPRDF), had almost gone to war with one of the major ethnic/religious parties, the Oromo Liberation Front (OLF). With the mediation of the U.S. embassy in Addis Ababa and other international players, war had been averted, but tensions were still high.

At the time, I was serving as economic and commercial officer at the embassy. My family and I could hear the sound of sporadic gunfire day and night. Rebel forces were terrorizing certain parts of the country. Even the embassy had been the target of a recent attack when someone threw a grenade over the compound wall. Fortunately, no one was injured, though there was some property damage.

As part of the mediated agreement with the EPRDF, the OLF agreed to encamp its bush fighters prior to local and regional elections. I was one of eight U.S. embassy employees who volunteered to participate as neutral international observers in the selection of campsites for these bush fighters. My job was to go to Ayana, a small village in northern Wellega province, with representatives from the OLF, the EPRDF, and the Eritrean People's Liberation Front (EPLF, the party of the Eritreans) to choose a campsite for OLF fighters in the area.

On Friday afternoon, April 17, in this uncertain and potentially dangerous environment, my group met at the military airport in Addis. An aging Soviet-made helicopter waited to transport us over the rugged Ethiopian highlands to our destination near the Blue Nile Gorge. I was concerned about the helicopter's state of disrepair, but even more worrisome were the representatives of the various factions that I was to accompany on this trip. Armed to the teeth and sporting scowls, they made me feel like I was going on a road trip seated between the Hatfields and McCoys. I closed my eyes and whispered a prayer as the helicopter left the ground.

The town of Ayana consisted of about 25 tin-roofed, adobe brick buildings along its one small, muddy street. I had reserved a room in the Ayana Hotel — the grandest building in town. Electricity was available a couple of hours each evening, but only if there was fuel to run the town generator. Most buildings in town had only naked light bulbs to take advantage of the power. The Ayana Hotel bar had the only television in town.

We arrived as the sun was setting. The hotel bar was filled with townsfolk eagerly watching whatever was showing on the one available channel. There was no indoor plumbing, no running water and no lights in the rooms. My "luxury" suite featured a cement floor, a bug-infested bed, and a candle stuck to a plastic dish. There was nothing between me and the sky except a thin sheet of corrugated tin. That night when it began to rain, I felt as if my head were stuck in a metal pail while somebody banged it with spoons.

The next day, within a matter of hours and way ahead of schedule, the rebel factions and I had located a suitable campsite for the OLF fighters only a few miles outside of town. What a relief. And not a shot fired. After a lunch of military rations, we wandered back to Ayana. I was pleased not only because we found a site so quickly, but also because I knew I'd be home in Addis Ababa by the next day, Easter Sunday, in time for dinner with my wife and two small children.

How wrong I was. The helicopter had already left and there was no way to contact EPRDF headquarters to let them know we were ready to go home. After four days of waiting, during which I visited every place in town, twice, a truck with a radio arrived. The next day a helicopter arrived. Because of a fuel shortage, we couldn't fly all the way back to the capital. Instead we ended up in another town, still several hours away from Addis by commercial air. There were no daily flights, so I waited another two days. My short trip to Ayana had turned into an eight-day ordeal.

I finally arrived home on a Saturday, just in time for a community party at the embassy. After a shower and a shave, I made my appearance at the celebration with family in tow. My colleagues greeted me with applause and whoops, as if I had risen from the dead. I later discovered that the seven other volunteers had been back for at least five days. No one had any idea what had happened to me.

Here's what I learned: In the Foreign Service, sometimes the job itself is easy. Getting there and back is the hard part.

Robert C. DeWitt served as an economic and commercial officer in Addis Ababa, Ethiopia, from 1991 to 1993. He joined the Foreign Service in 1991 and has served in Kampala, Uganda; Beijing, China; Quito, Ecuador; and Shanghai, China.

Passing the Keys
MOZAMBIQUE, 1990
By Daniel Hirsch

In the late 1980s, the president of Mozambique, Joaquim Chissano, wanted to improve relations with other countries, and especially with the Vatican. The Vatican told him something like this: "Return to the churches all properties that your government took from them; then we'll talk." This was something that the U.S. also supported.

Chissano found native representatives for almost every religious group: Catholics, Protestants, Muslims, etc., and returned to them the keys to all churches, mosques and related buildings and cemeteries. But he could not find, anywhere in Mozambique, a Jew. There was a synagogue and a Jewish cemetery in Maputo, and he did not know to whom to return them. He eventually discovered that the U.S. embassy's deputy chief of mission, Michael Metelits, was Jewish. After some deliberation on both sides, Chissano "returned" the synagogue and the Jewish cemetery to him.

The synagogue had been used over the years as a military depot, a brothel, and a dump, and required considerable repair. The cemetery had been vandalized and was occupied by squatters. Over the next few months (the rest of his tour there), Michael volunteered considerable time to raise funds (primarily from the South African Jewish community) for repair works, which began, under the supervision of a local businessman, before he left Maputo.

When Michael left Maputo, he left me (the only other known Jew in the country) the keys. As the work progressed, various people came out of the woodwork. People noticed that somebody was working on the synagogue, asked the workmen what was going on, and were eventually directed to me. Within a few months, about a dozen people had shown up, with essentially the same story: they had been born Jewish, but raised during the colonial or communist period without any knowledge of their religion. So in my spare time, I started ed a weekly class to teach them the basics. For the next year, I served as the informal "rabbi" of the synagogue in Maputo, and led the group through a single year of Jewish holidays. By the time I left, the group had come together, had been recognized by Mozambique's Ministry of Culture and Religion, and elected a leader from among themselves. They had also arranged for a South African rabbi to visit Maputo regularly and "minister" to them.

Not long ago, at the Takoma Park Street Festival outside Washington, D.C., I saw someone raising money to benefit small Jewish communities around the world, including the Maputo Jewish community. He had pictures of the synagogue and some of the community members. Without knowing the names, he told me the story I have just told here. I donated $50, and moved on.

Daniel Hirsch was general services officer in Maputo, Mozambique, from 1990 to 1992. He joined the Foreign Service in 1985 and he has also served in Bamako, Mali; Praia, Cape Verde; Bissau, Guinea-Bissau; Tashkent, Uzbekistan; Abuja, Nigeria; Calcutta, India; Bishkek, Kyrgyzstan; Belgrade, Serbia; and Ashgabat, Turkmenistan.

All the Leaves Are Gone
BANGLADESH, 1991
By Mary Kilgour

Our plane landed in Chittagong, two days after the April 1991 cyclone. Sergeant Jeffrey Kern from the defense attaché's office, Lieutenant Jason Carver (on temporary assignment under the civic action program), and I (the USAID mission director) were to inspect the damage and report back to the ambassador in Dhaka.

We hurried to the makeshift waiting area. A Bangladesh Army officer, Captain Ali, took us for a briefing and a city tour. Farms were covered with sea water; wooden buildings were piles of scrap; a barge blocked an inland road.

Vendors were spreading their goods to dry on the ground, in the rain. The smell of rot was everywhere. Children picked through the

All the leaves are gone.

debris for something to eat. Dead humans and animals lay face down in the water among weeds, pieces of buildings, and plastic bags.

Huge cranes had toppled; warehouses had crumpled. We visited a Navy ship that had been tied up during the cyclone. The captain showed us the barograph that traced the fall of atmospheric pressure as the cyclone approached: off the graph.

I went to city hall to present the mayor with water purification tablets. He pointed out a window. "Look. All the leaves are gone. The wind and rain ripped the trees bare, just as they have taken away our loved ones, our livelihoods." He closed his eyes and tears coursed down his cheeks.

In the evening, I ate rice and lentils with him and other civilians at a hotel illuminated by candles. The conversation never strayed from the cyclone and each survivor's terrible story.

The hotel was full and no plane was flying that night, but a train was returning to Dhaka. Word came that a space had been arranged for me. An hour later, a Bangladeshi ensign arrived to escort me to the train station. We made our way through disorder, blackness and driving rain. The ensign took his assignment seriously, inquiring about my work and life and volunteering similar information.

We arrived at the station and followed the jeep's headlights to the entrance. Inside, the ensign led me by the hand through the pitch-black waiting room. People were sleeping everywhere. We had to walk on them to get to the platform. I felt the bodies wriggling underfoot but they made no sound.

The ensign pulled at my hand. "Keep moving."

At the train, he thanked me. "I enjoyed our conversation. If I visit Dhaka, can I call on you? I would like to introduce you to my parents."

Was this a Fellini film? I heard myself saying, "You're not leaving me, are you?"

He took my hand again. "No, I won't leave until your companions arrive."

How silly I must have seemed, worrying about my safety among sleeping refugees. But that wasn't my fear. It had more to do with the displacement of order.

Jason and Jeff arrived. We boarded the train and found our accommodations. I was so tired that I fell asleep immediately.

Boats washed inland by tidal surge.

I awoke early to overwhelming silence and stillness, and lay thinking about the horrors of the day.

The sky lightened. The train started moving. Jeff knocked on the door. "Want to join us for breakfast?"

"You have food?"

"Meals Ready to Eat. You're welcome to share."

We split two MREs between us. The attendant provided bottled water. I found myself abnormally happy to be with them.

Jason had been about to leave when the cyclone struck. "I'm going to have to stay and help. Repairing the airport terminal might be useful."

"USAID can provide grants to some of the relief organizations to distribute shelter repair materials, and we can divert food aid already in country to relief purposes," I said.

"I think the colonel will recommend bringing in more military assets," Jeff said. His boss would be visiting Chittagong himself.

It was daylight now. We had spent the night on a sidetrack just outside Chittagong, the conductor said. We would reach Dhaka in late afternoon.

Together, Jason, Jeff and I would tell the ambassador what we had seen and heard, and offer recommendations for a U.S. response. Then we would work as hard as we could until the worst was over.

By the end of our labor, we learned that this Category 5 cyclone, called Marion, had killed 139,000 people and a million animals in six hours.

Mary Cameron Kilgour was USAID mission director in Dhaka, Bangladesh, from 1990 to 1993. She joined the Foreign Service in 1966 and retired in 1995. She served in Lahore and Islamabad, Pakistan; Bogota, Colombia; San Jose, Costa Rica; Manila, Philippines; and Monrovia, Liberia. She now lives in Gainesville, Florida, where she writes fiction and memoirs (her childhood memoir was published in 2004) and volunteers with Habitat for Humanity and the Guardian ad Litem program.

The Crash of Flight 965
COLOMBIA, 1995
By Michael Jacobsen

Late in the evening of December 20, 1995, the holiday spirit at U.S. Embassy Bogota was shattered when American Airlines Flight 965 crashed high in the Andes Mountains in southwestern Colombia, killing 164 passengers and crew members, including 63 Americans. Vice Consul Robyn Hooker called me at home at about 10 p.m. to say that CNN was reporting a plane crash near the city of Cali. The following days and nights would be like nothing I had lived through thus far in my Foreign Service career.

I was no stranger to the fragility of life in Colombia; I had lived with a Colombian host family and traveled extensively there while a university exchange student in 1978. I had recently returned to Colombia, as the chief of the American citizen services unit.

Within hours of the crash, and following a quick strategy session over the phone with Consul General Jean Louis, an embassy team that included Vice Consul Ray Kengott and myself was descending quickly over the Cauca Valley on the embassy's Drug Enforcement Administration plane. Ray and I settled on a working priority: we would keep compassion for the victims' families uppermost in the midst of the chaos that we were sure to find at the crash site.

Once in the airport, we struggled to obtain a copy of the passenger list from "locked" airline computers and began relaying the names to the embassy working group, which in turn was feeding updates to anxious family members and to State Department colleagues who had formed their own task force in the Operations Center in Washington.

As dawn broke over the valley, we headed north to the small town of Buga, headquarters for Colombia's Third Army Brigade, which was located at the base of the heavily forested, guerrilla-infested mountaintop crash site. Working our way through the semi-controlled chaos of the base, we managed to hop into one of the army's Huey helicopters that were ferrying rescue crews to the crash site. The helicopter rose slowly toward the site of this horrific tragedy.

Circling around the top of the 9,000-foot mountain, we could see a jagged treeless scar that ran a few hundred feet up one side of the peak and shredded back down the other for about the same distance. It seemed the pilots of Flight 965 had almost managed to clear the mountain as they climbed desperately higher but that on impact, the plane had barreled up and over the peak before skidding to a halt in thick jungle growth on the other side. Ribbons of clothing were scattered across the treetops. We learned later that guerrillas and other looters had fled overnight with all but about six of the hundreds of suitcases, cargo and Christmas gifts thrown clear of the plane, while not daring to touch the victims themselves.

Over the next several days, driving rain and cold temperatures on the mountain limited the search for bodies by the determined Colombian military and civilian rescue teams to a few hours each day. Meanwhile, consular reinforcements from the embassy in Bogota, the State Department, and three other embassies in the region began arriving. One group staffed a command center at one of Cali's prominent hotels to receive incoming family members of the victims, while another worked out of an office on the premises of Buga's main sports facility, designated by the Colombian authorities as the temporary morgue.

At our recommendation, U.S. Ambassador Myles Frechette intervened with high-ranking Colombian government officials to ensure security in Buga was adequate and to persuade them to allow a team of FBI forensics experts to assist with the identification of the remains. Completing our preparations with the support of administrative colleagues Cliff Tighe and Larry Kay, we located a decent hotel in Buga to shelter our onsite consular team, moved into the small office space close to the indoor gym, and made the necessary working contacts with local officials by the time the first remains were brought down from the mountaintop on the morning of the second day after the accident.

Fortunately, most of the victims' bodies, though badly mangled, were still relatively intact and therefore identifiable. Under the guidance of Embassy Bogota's senior Colombian consular employee, Maria Cristina Gomez, members of our team worked from early morning until late into the night through the Christmas holidays assisting family members confirm identifications and preparing all documentation needed for burial of the victims in Colombia or repatriation of the remains to the U.S. We held daily meetings with our official Colombian counterparts to arrange for recovery of personal effects and to insist that the search continue until all Americans had been found.

The next few days have now become a blur, but certain moments remain vivid in the mind's eye: a Colombian rescue worker, silently surrounded by several of his colleagues, sitting on the ground rocking slowly back and forth while cradling the blanketed corpse of the youngest victim, a 1-year-old American boy; a promise to a distraught American father that I would not permit the search to end until his daughter's body was recovered — a promise we kept; a visit to the four survivors of the crash in the hospital, who described their near-death experiences; Deputy Secretary of State Strobe Talbott's call to me on Christmas Day to express his appreciation for our efforts.

Ten days after the crash, on December 30, 1995, I departed Cali under a warm morning sun, climbing up over the Cauca Valley's vast sugar cane fields aboard the DEA plane with the remaining members of the embassy relief team. We left with a commitment from the Colombian government and a pledge to an American family that the search would not end until the last victim, a 9-year-old American boy, was found — his remains were located several days later.

Exactly one year later, as Jean and I sat with the American and Colombian family members resident in Cali who were holding a memorial mass for the victims of Flight 965, I felt satisfied that the U.S. government had succeeded in shining a guiding and comforting light for these families during a time of unbearable loss.

Michael Jacobsen was chief of the American citizen services unit in Bogota, Colombia, from 1995 to 1998. He joined the Foreign Service in 1986, and has served in Santo Domingo, Dominican Republic; Montevideo, Uruguay; Washington, D.C.; Manila, Philippines; Bogota, Colombia; Bangkok, Thailand; and Guatemala City, Guatemala.

That's Classified!
UZBEKISTAN, 2000
By Barbara Jacquin

As a State Department diplomatic courier, it's my job to make sure America's classified documents are shipped around the world safely. "Dip" couriers are some of the world's most frequent fliers, yet most people don't even know we exist, let alone hear about our adventures and challenges. Like the time I flew into Uzbekistan…

Somewhere over the Caspian Sea, approaching Almaty, Kazakhstan. Dead of winter. It is 9:30 p.m. local time. The purser announces that snow on the runway prevents us from landing. We must land in Tashkent, Uzbekistan, and spend the night in a hotel. I find the purser and inform him that my responsibility is to remain with my pouches, loaded in a giant container in the airplane's belly. There are consultations with the pilot. In the meantime, Embassy Tashkent is informed that I'm here and may or may not need help. Imagine the embassy duty officer's enthusiasm to

Ensuring that all pouches are accounted for and loaded on the plane in Vienna.

come out to the airport and sit all night in a car with me, staring at the cargo door of an Airbus 340 in sub-zero weather!

Someone performs a miracle and I am allowed to sleep alone in the plane with the small concession of having a security guard in and around the plane during the night. The pilot shows me how to open and close the big door leading out to the stairs and bids me farewell ... for a time. I later agree with the guard that we don't really need the humming auxiliary power on. He stops it, and the plane begins to settle — snap, crackle, and pop! Ah, the comforting sounds of home.

A few hours later, dawn comes and brings a gaggle of uniformed guards: security, army, who knows? They stamp all our passports and begin to search the entire plane — overhead bins, seat cushions, and pockets behind seat backs. I realize they are probably looking for drugs since many pass through this region. No one bothers me, though I hear them whispering about "the diplomatic courier." Eventually the crew arrives, followed by the well-rested and well-fed passengers, all inquiring into my well-being after spending the night alone on the plane.

Finally we are airborne for Almaty by 11 a.m. I have to admit that even though I'm hungry and need a shower, it wasn't such a bad experience after all. At least I wasn't sleeping on top of my pouches in some cold warehouse — a pleasure a few of my fellow couriers have had.

Diplomatic couriers are no longer chained by the wrist to their pouches like Tyrone Power in the classic film "Diplomatic Courier," but they are conscious every second of the location of their loads. Whether containers in the belly of an airplane, loose-loaded pieces in the baggage compartment or simply a small piece in their briefcase, couriers know precisely where the diplomatic pouches are at all times.

Have you noticed the passenger who always arrives last on the plane or the passenger who jumps out of his seat like a jack-in-the-box the second the plane arrives at the gate and the seat-belt sign goes off? If so, you've probably observed a courier in action.

Couriers have an exciting, but sometimes lonely, job. We travel all the time, spending numerous hours waiting under planes for the loading to end or the unloading to begin. In our time off, we find ourselves alone exploring new and exotic cities. We are all incurable tourists.

So, if you ever find yourself sitting next to a dip courier on a plane, you have the opportunity of a lifetime to hear some great tales from a veteran traveler. But whatever you do, don't ask what's inside the pouch — that's classified!

Barbara Jacquin has been posted to Belgrade, Yugoslavia; Suva, Fiji; Mbabane, Swaziland; Ouagadougou, Burkina Faso; Port-au-Prince, Haiti; and the Frankfurt Regional Courier Office in Germany. She dedicates this story to Seth Foti, a courier who perished in the line of duty in August 2000.

The Evacuation
PAKISTAN, 1998
By Scott Rauland

My family and I were evacuated from Pakistan in August of 1998 in the wake of the U.S. embassy bombings in Kenya and Tanzania. It has proven to be the most difficult experience we have had in the Foreign Service to date. I had gone to Islamabad in April 1998 ahead of my family to fill a slot as American Center director that had been vacant almost a year. My wife and children stayed in Berlin to finish the school year, then made a visit to the U.S. to see relatives before finally arriving in Islamabad August 10.

We were just getting settled into our house, newly reunited as a family, and had taken the children (ages 11 and 8 at the time) to the International School of Islamabad for their orientation August 14. My son and daughter were both excited about making new friends and learning more about Islamabad, which I had described to them through letters and photos for over four months.

At about midnight on August 17, the night before school started, the doorbell rang. I muttered several less-than-diplomatic oaths under my breath, wondering why the residential security guard was disturbing us at that time of night. He handed me an embassy security bulletin, and in my groggy state I read something about a security threat and an ordered departure. After a few more minutes it finally made sense to me — all spouses, children, and non-essential embassy staff (including me) were being asked to make preparations the following day (Monday) to leave Pakistan at the crack of dawn on Tuesday, August 19, on an evacuation of undetermined length. I remember letting out a howl of anger and frustration, then returning to our bedroom to deliver the bad news to my wife.

Our most difficult decision that evening was whether to allow the children to go to school for the first and likely their only school day of that fall semester, uncertain whether they would ever return to Islamabad. We allowed them to go, in the hope that the evacuation would not last long and that they would have memories of teachers and fellow students they could look forward to seeing again someday. Watching them get on the bus that next morning was one of the most bittersweet memories of my life.

We traveled back to the U.S. together on a series of chartered flights. The entire trip took more than 24 hours with many long stops on the way. After getting the family settled in Wisconsin, I continued to Washington, D.C., where I worked for about a month. After five weeks I was allowed to return to my job at post — but without my family — for the duration of the evacuation.

The evacuation for dependents and some non-essential personnel lasted five long months. The worst part was the sense that our lives were permanently on hold, never knowing for sure when we would see each other again. One of the most poignant memories I have of my children's reaction to the experience of living out of a suitcase for five months was the difficulty they had establishing friendships. As one of my son's school acquaintances put it when he had been invited to come over and play, "Why would I want to come to your house? You don't have anything and there is nothing to do!"

We were ultimately reunited in late January, and went on to have a very memorable tour in Pakistan. Since our departure in 2000, Embassy Islamabad has been under evacuation orders twice, one evacuation lasting almost a year. Evacuations are a fact of life in the Foreign Service and Foreign Service employees and their families face hardships that make a mockery of the stereotypical notion that our careers revolve around endless receptions of tea and cookies.

Scott Rauland was the American Center director in Islamabad from 1998 to 2000. He joined the Foreign Service in 1993 and his other postings have been to Baku, Azerbaijan; Berlin, Germany; and Quito, Ecuador.

Leave No American Behind
MACEDONIA, 2001
By Bix Aliu

From the first shots fired on a police station in early March 2001 to the signing of the Western-brokered Framework Agreement in August 2001, Macedonia was engulfed in a violent conflict pitting armed insurgents against government forces. In the emergency operations that summer at Embassy Skopje, the deeds of one junior consular officer stand out: Glenn Nye worked tirelessly, devising innovative solutions that drew on all the embassy's resources to handle two life-threatening situations and bring 27 Americans to safety.

After the embassy was attacked by a rock-throwing mob one evening, an emergency detachment of Marines came to secure the chancery. At the same time, the safety of private Americans living in western Macedonia was threatened as the area came under control of armed insurgents who closed the roads and set up armed checkpoints. A large group of Americans was stranded between two villages in northwest Macedonia. The embassy knew they were there, but all phone connections to the villages were cut.

Glenn Nye (left) with a group of American evacuees safely removed from Vratnice.

Believing the area probably had cell-phone coverage, Glenn decided that there was a chance to reach Americans there through local political contacts. He went immediately to the political section and pooled ideas with me. We got the phone number of a political activist living in the crisis area. By using that link and expanding it out to a network of local cell numbers, Glenn was able to organize the identification of all the Americans who needed to be evacuated.

Glenn then quickly worked with the embassy refugee coordinator to contract a bus driver willing to enter the area to pick up the Americans at a rally point. He negotiated with a local mayor, who had the only working car in the area, to personally bring one elderly American couple down from a remote village to the bus. The mayor reported that there was a window of time when the road would be clear, and the bus was coordinated to get all the Americans out safely to Skopje during that window.

At that point only one crisis remained: the insurgent group had captured an American citizen, along with several locals, and was holding them hostage. Earlier efforts to secure release of the hostages had failed. Glenn took over primary responsibility for working to free the American hostage. Though he was constrained by the policy of not negotiating for hostages, he set out a course of action to raise the pressure on the insurgents. Glenn used political contacts he had established over the preceding year to get the word indirectly to the insurgents that one of their units held an American citizen and that the U.S. government would not tolerate the act. Glenn convinced the insurgents to let him have phone contact with the hostage.

During a brief conversation, Glenn confirmed the identity of the American hostage, established for the first time since his disappearance that he was still alive, and determined his location. He finally had key information to pass on to the despondent family in the United States, and the ability to step up his campaign with precisely targeted messages to the insurgents.

The pressure paid off. Glenn received a call informing him that the American prisoner's release would occur immediately, and shortly thereafter, the Red Cross received a call telling them they could come pick up the hostages. After a medical check and a healthy meal, the American was on a flight home the next day to rejoin a tearful but relieved family.

Bix Aliu served in Skopje from 1997 to 2001, the last three months as special assistant to the ambassador. He joined the Foreign Service in 1997, and has also served as vice consul in Dubai, United Arab Emirates.

Seven Days in Kerala
INDIA, 2000
By Alejandro "Hoot" Baez

It was the spring of 2000 and my first Foreign Service tour, as a junior officer vice consul at the U.S. consulate in Chennai, India, was drawing to a close. Mahesh, an Indian staff member in the immigrant visa unit, and I were embarking on a weeklong journey around the consular district to investigate suspected immigration fraud cases. We flew from Chennai to Cochin, a lovely little town in the state of Kerala on the Arabian Sea.

First on my schedule was a visa policy speech. U.S. immigration and visa policy is a mystery to many Indians. Often our decisions are viewed as arbitrary — or worse. As a result, the consulate had launched a proactive public diplomacy campaign, encouraging officers to give speeches explaining the factors used in determining U.S. visa eligibility. I had arranged to give one of these speeches in Cochin. The audience's thirst for knowledge about the subject was so great — and the questions so numerous — that my presentation lasted four hours.

After the speech, the local leaders of the Indo-American Chamber of Commerce hosted a dinner in my honor. They presented their views on the growing economic and political ties between our two countries. They also offered a few complaints about certain U.S. policies.

The next morning Mahesh and I rose early to begin our fraud investigations. Over the course of the week, we completed 21 investigations and found fraud in 13 of these cases. Under U.S. immigration law, the individuals involved in these 13 cases would be permanently barred from traveling to the United States.

Our investigative approach depended on the specifics of each case. If a case rested on the validity of an applicant's claim to have married an American at a particular church in Kerala, we went to that church, talked with the priest, and checked the marriage records. If no record existed, we knew the marriage was a sham.

Two days into our investigations, we had to dramatically shift gears. After a long day of investigations, Mahesh and I arrived at our hotel at 8 p.m. and found a message waiting for us: "Call the consulate." The consular section chief told me he had heard from the parents of a young man who had been traveling in South India. The young man had not called home in several weeks, and his parents were worried. Their concern was compounded by the fact that the son had a history of mental illness and drug abuse. The consulate's American citizen services unit had succeeded in tracking down the young man's location, a hotel in Cochin.

My job was to go to his hotel, check on his condition, and ask him to call his folks. I grabbed a taxi and headed to his hotel. Unfortunately, the hotel had recently kicked him out. He had not paid his bill in several days, and had been acting erratically. I explained to the hotel's manager who I was, and he offered to help me find the young man.

Eventually, we found him down on the wharf. Not only had he run out of money, he had also stopped taking his medication, which explained the erratic behavior observed by the hotel staff. When I first introduced myself to the young American, he made it clear that the last thing he wanted to do was to talk to me or to his family. I spent the next several hours on the rat-infested dock trying to win his confidence. In time, I was able to check him into another hotel, persuade him to start taking his medicine again, set up a phone call to his parents, and arrange for his parents to wire him some money. I finally tumbled into my own bed at 2 a.m.

Later in the week, another American citizen services case came my way. An American had died in the city of Trivandrum several weeks earlier, and the local police were holding his personal effects. I spent several hours in the police station carefully conducting an inventory of his belongings. I then took possession of them and forwarded them to his family in the United States. One item was an expensive wheelchair, which, at his family's request, I donated to a local charity.

As my time in Kerala drew to a close, I was exhausted and invigorated. The week had been a perfect encapsulation of my tour in India. I was more certain than ever in the wisdom of my decision to join the Foreign Service.

Alejandro Baez was a consular officer in Chennai from 1998 to 2000. He joined the Foreign Service in 1998. From Chennai, he went on to an assignment as a political officer at Embassy Moscow.

Rats and Resourcefulness
PHILIPPINES, 1987
By Jim Wagner

In 1987, I was a low-ranking political officer assigned to the consulate in Cebu, Philippines. My beat was the southern Philippines, the Visayas to Mindanao. Trips to the more remote places were like comic-book quests: the only way to approach them was with the spirit of an adventurer, relaxed and prepared at all times for the unexpected.

One such journey was to conduct a pulse-check on political and economic conditions in a rural zone in northeastern Mindanao. I landed on the dirt-strip runway in the provincial capital just as a tropical storm hit. Even in the best of weather, the only ground transportation to town was a motorcycle with a creatively jerry-rigged sidecar. Asking the motorcyclist for a hotel, I was met with a nonchalant "No hotel." I ended up at a miserable rooming house whose rates included towel rentals.

Depositing my bag, I made for the provincial governor's office, my usual first stop on reporting jaunts. The governor, a pleasant woman with an avowed love of the new government in Manila, welcomed my unannounced arrival. Her first question was about my lodging. Learning where I was staying, she told me that I would be a guest at her home and without waiting for my answer, dispatched her personal secretary (who happened to be her son) to retrieve my bag.

I spent the rest of the day talking with various locals: Catholic Church officials, a bank manager, the mayor, and the military commander. Hoping to get a feel for the security climate in this area bordering a known communist guerilla zone, but instead hearing a lot of griping about being a backwater province ignored by the capital, I made my way to the governor's home — a two-story cinder-block house set on a dirt street.

The thing one notices about provincial life in the Philippines is the unceasing noise from machines sorely needing tune-ups — the roar of muffler-less motorcycles and the hum of generators powering the houses of the fortunate few well-off enough to afford them. The governor's home was no exception. After being shown the guest room — complete with just-like-in-the-movies mosquito netting — I joined Mrs. Governor in her living room as dinner preparations were under way.

Sitting across from me on a sofa, the governor held forth on how to improve things in her province. Midway through one thought, but unnoticed by her, a rat wandered out from under the sofa. Not a mouse. A rat. The rat obviously felt at home since he was in no hurry to find a hiding place, but instead stared at me, the stranger. My mind turned to those etiquette lessons we received in basic training. Should I inform the hostess about the rat? Or keep up the conversation as if it were the most natural occurrence? I opted for the latter. The rat strolled back under the sofa. I don't remember what was served for dinner.

Night was quiet; all the generators were shut down by 9 p.m. to conserve resources.

The next day, Mrs. Governor insisted that I borrow a car and driver from the provincial motor pool to make my way to the neighboring province. That particular area of the Philippines was dense jungle and known for occasional reptile-native encounters, so I accepted. After crossing a bridge into a peninsula-like area that was part of our northbound journey, the driver informed me that we were lucky since the span would be closed at noon for several days of repairs.

Hours and kilometers later, we neared the only other vehicle bridge that crossed back to the mainland and led on to the neighboring province to the northwest. The tropical storm had blown out the bridge. The ever-resourceful driver recalled that a new bridge was under construction downstream and, with luck, it would be finished. It wasn't. It was my turn to be resourceful. Spying a crane, I negotiated a deal with the workers — lift and pass the car from bank to bank for the equivalent of $60. To the delight of the gathering crowd, the feat was accomplished in less than one hour and with no damage to the car. (I opted for the footbridge.)

That evening, in my room in the half-star hotel in the capital of this neighboring province, jotting in my notebook how much of the Philippines still remained isolated pockets of natural beauty and human misery, I marveled at the day's events. That is, until I was stricken with the worst case of dysentery I have had in my Foreign

Service career — just as the lights and water were being shut down for the night to conserve resources.

Jim Wagner was a political officer at the U.S. consulate in Cebu from 1986 to 1988. He joined the Foreign Service in 1981, and has also served in Managua, Nicaragua; Madrid, Spain; Caracas, Venezuela; Lima, Peru; Brussels, Belgium (at the U.S. Mission to the European Union) and Washington, D.C.

Heathrow Airport on September 12
UNITED KINGDOM, 2001
By Eric Fichte

It was Wednesday evening, September 12, 2001, at Heathrow Airport, where several hundred Americans were stranded. Two consular officers had been dispatched with instructions to figure out what was going on, do what they could to settle these people for the night, and make sure accurate information was being disseminated. I was one of them.

"The only television they have in this place is in the bar," he said, sounding annoyed.

"I'm sorry about that, sir," I replied. "I'm happy to tell you as much as the embassy knows."

"Yeah, yeah. I want to know one positive thing you guys have done. One positive thing," he said, issuing the challenge, confident the odds were in his favor.

"We've convinced an airline to change its policy and put stranded Americans in hotels, negotiated with hotels to offer reduced rates for American citizens, helped countless stranded travelers find lodging, and filled prescriptions for stranded Americans with health conditions."

"Oh," he said, and headed back to the bar.

The terminal was a zoo. Over 200 people were piled into a lounge, bodies crammed into corners or bent at odd angles to create the semblance of a flat surface. Faces peered out from behind piles of luggage. Airport representatives, exasperated that the airlines had not done so all day, fed the masses. Hands reached into food boxes stacked precariously on hand trolleys. Small bags of potato chips and bottles of mineral water sailed through the air. Dinner was finally served.

Misinformation was king. Uncertainty and doubt ruled. Some airline representatives sent passengers directly to hotels; others told people to check back every 15 minutes. Meanwhile, some airlines were checking baggage and issuing boarding passes for phantom flights. And into this mess flew a constant stream of incoming flights, all delivering more bodies, more statistical robustness, to the equation.

Our task was straightforward: inform as many people as possible about what we knew and what we expected, and assist as much as possible with what to do in the meantime. While we didn't have much hard information, close consultation with embassy FAA representatives allowed us to provide a realistic assessment of the next 48 hours. A resumption of flights was highly unlikely. We had to make that clear.

Passing the word turned out to be much easier than initially feared. Instead of anger, we saw gratitude when we told passengers they would probably not fly for at least a couple of days. People didn't mind hearing bad news, just so long as they received an honest assessment of what they faced. Perhaps some airlines set the stage by building expectations to unreasonable levels. Or perhaps most everyone traveling understood that while they had been inconvenienced, the true tragedy was in the United States.

As we worked our way through the terminal, talking to as many Americans as we could find, another amazing event unfolded before us. Private American citizens, having heard about the stranded passengers, descended on the airport to open their homes and their hearts. Amid the confusion, we now had a terrific tonic — compassion.

For the next two days, we repeated our message. Tempers shortened slightly and emotions surfaced quicker for all involved, but the peace held and we were still able to make a difference. We filled prescriptions for stranded Americans with health concerns, negotiated reduced rates at area hotels for Americans, helped organize and coordinate our private citizens' efforts, pointed people in the right direction and — above every thing else — spoke in a frank and straightforward manner. It was the least we could do.

Eric Fichte was a consular officer in London from 2000 to 2002. Before joining the Foreign Service, he worked for the State Department in the Freedom of Information Act office and as a consular associate in Matamoros, Mexico. He joined the Foreign Service in 1997 and has served in Paramaribo, Suriname, and the State Department Operations Center in Washington.

Paving the Way for Women
DEPARTMENT OF STATE, 2002
By Phyllis E. Oakley

I am constantly amazed at the changes in women's demeanor as I walk through the State Department. Today's female Foreign Service officers look sharp, determined, and confident, a far cry from what I remember of myself and a few intrepid friends from graduate school when we dared to brave the male bastion that was the 1957 Foreign Service. Indeed, I was the only woman in my orientation class of 30.

I recall how I felt at that time, not quite sure how I would be treated and as something of an interloper, a brazen intruder, if you will, trying to put a female presence in the Foreign Service, a career so clearly dominated and controlled by men. Then I did exactly what had been foretold would happen if the Foreign Service started to accept more women: I met and became engaged to another FSO. My consciousness being at the prevailing low level of the time, it did not occur to me to protest or fight the unspoken rule that required women officers who married to resign their positions. And so I resigned, prepared my trousseau, wed

Bob Oakley in Cairo — thanks to a one-way ticket from my father — and we started our great adventure to his postings in the Sudan, Ivory Coast (with two children in tow), Vietnam, Paris, New York, and Beirut.

By then, it was the early 1970s, and America was changing. There was a sexual revolution, a feminist revolution, and a political revolution — thanks to Vietnam. Even the State Department changed. To avoid discrimination lawsuits, in 1974 the State Department offered re-entry to women like me, former female FSOs who might choose to return to the Foreign Service.

I found it a great advantage to be a woman in the mid-1970s. Officials were striving to advance women and to demonstrate that they were moving with the times. I became the first female staff assistant on the seventh floor, where the highest-level State officials work. I was the first spouse permitted to work in her husband's embassy (in Kinshasa), and the first spokeswoman in the State Department. It was a rewarding path — providing both time for my children when they were young and a fulfilling career.

Entering classes of the Foreign Service now often have a majority of women. One sees women in meetings presenting their views without a hint of deferral to men or a desire to hold back. Sessions where women dominate and sometimes make up the entire staff are commonplace. And tandem couples — in which both spouses are FSOs — have become ordinary.

I hope young officers starting careers today will remember that most of the changes for women at the State Department would not have come about without lawsuits and a fair amount of pushing. An Equal Employment Opportunity Commission complaint was filed early on and a class action lawsuit was initiated in the mid-1970s by female State Department employees alleging discrimination on assignments, promotions, and awards. In 1987, after a laborious process, the U.S. District Court for the District of Columbia found in the women's favor.

Both men and women in the Foreign Service today should know that the tension between career and parenthood still exists, especially for women. The decision of the U.S. ambassador to Pakistan, Wendy Chamberlin, to curtail her assignment to that strategic post because she is a single mother and her two teenage girls were forced to evacuate — twice — highlights this problem. No matter what, working mothers still have hard choices to make.

Would I recommend the Foreign Service career to young women today? You bet I would. In spite of the danger, sharp shards left in the breached glass ceiling, and complexities of family life, I still see the Foreign Service as the most interesting and worthwhile career in the world. I am pleased that so many outstanding young people still seem to agree.

Phyllis E. Oakley rejoined the Foreign Service in 1974 and retired in 1999. She was one of the first women appointed to high-level management in the State Department. She served as State's Deputy Spokesman from 1986 to 1989, as Assistant Secretary of the Bureau of Intelligence and Research, and as Assistant Secretary of the Bureau of Population, Refugees, and Migration. Her overseas postings were to Kinshasa, Zaire, and Islamabad, Pakistan.

Tie A Yellow Ribbon
IRAN, 1981
By L. Bruce Laingen

For me, to look back on almost 40 years in the Foreign Service is to see a kaleidoscope of experiences that a farm boy from Minnesota could not conceivably have imagined: issuing visas, at times around the clock, at a displaced persons camp in postwar Germany; flying the U.S. flag as consul in a listening post at Meshed, close to the then-Soviet border of Iran; escorting First Lady Jackie Kennedy on her 1962 triumphal tour of Pakistan; watching President Lyndon Johnson invite Anwar, the Pakistani camel driver, to visit the United States; observing the India-Pakistan War of 1971 that saw the birth of Bangladesh; and sailing in the magnificent Grand Harbor of the island republic of Malta.

But one assignment is etched forever in my mind: my second tour in Iran, in 1979-81, when I became a candidate for the Guinness Book of Records — the only chief of a diplomatic mission to lose his embassy and its entire staff to political terrorists supported by their government, and to be held hostage for political purposes for more than a year. This was arguably the most egregious violation of the traditions and principles of diplomatic immunity in history.

In America's experience with the Iranian revolution that began in 1979, there are volumes of remembrances — and lessons: the need in times of political uncertainty to challenge conventional wisdom; my staff's endurance with dignity; the heroism and sacrifice of those men who put their lives on the line to restore us hostages to freedom but whose flying machines failed them; and being reminded of our good fortune in a neighbor, Canada, which was ready to set aside all its interests in Iran to bring six Americans home to safety.

But perhaps we should remember the way this crisis also triggered what became a class act of the best of community across our country. Beginning with an understandable outburst of anger and hate, much of it unfortunately directed at Iranians living in America, there evolved a most remarkable spirit of national unity — an outpouring of caring symbolized by flags, prayers, church bells, an avalanche of mail, and above all that ubiquitous yellow ribbon, which became and remains today the universal symbol of caring for fellow Americans in distress.

For a time, at least, there was also a new appreciation by the American public of the role played by their diplomats abroad in areas of stress and danger. Since then others in the Foreign Service have continued that role, often on the front lines in defense of American interests — in Beirut, Kuwait, Somalia, Nairobi, Dar es Salaam — and today, in new countries born of the former Soviet Union, of whose freedom my Foreign Service generation could only dream 50 years ago. Today I tell all who are new to the Foreign Service: Welcome to the ultimate in adventure, and in public service.

L. Bruce Laingen served as chief of mission in Tehran, Iran, from 1979 to 1981. He retired from the Foreign Service in 1987. In his 38-year career, he also served in Hamburg, Germany; Washington, D.C; Karachi, Pakistan; Kabul, Afghanistan; and as ambassador to Valletta, Malta. He is currently serving as president of the American Academy of Diplomacy.

Acronyms and Abbreviations

ADB	Asian Development Bank
AFSA	American Foreign Service Association
APEC	Asia Pacific Economic Cooperation
ASEAN	Association of Southeast Asian Nations
CA	Consular Affairs, also Consular Agency
CDC	Centers for Disease Control and Prevention
CIA	Central Intelligence Agency
CODEL	Congressional Delegation (from Washington)
DEA	Drug Enforcement Administration
DAO	Defense Attaché Office
DOD	Department of Defense
EPA	Environmental Protection Agency
FAA	Federal Aviation Administration
FAS	Foreign Agricultural Service
FBI	Federal Bureau of Investigation
FBIS	Foreign Broadcast Information Service
FCS	Foreign Commercial Service
FS	Foreign Service
FSI	Foreign Service Institute, also called NFATC
GAO	General Accounting Office
HHS	Department of Health and Human Services
HR	Human Resources
IBB	International Broadcasting Bureau
IMET	International Military Education and Training
IMF	International Monetary Fund
INS	Immigration and Naturalization Service
IRS	Internal Revenue Service
IV	Immigrant Visa
JCS	Joint Chiefs of Staff
NAFTA	North American Free Trade Agreement
NASA	National Aeronautics and Space Administration
NATO	North Atlantic Treaty Organization
NFATC	National Foreign Affairs Training Center, usually called FSI
NIV	Non-Immigrant Visa
NGO	Non-Governmental Organization
NSC	National Security Council
OAS	Organization of American States
OECD	Organization for Economic Cooperation and Development
OFDA	Office of Foreign Disaster Assistance
OPIC	Overseas Private Investment Corporation
OSCE	Organization for Security and Cooperation in Europe
PA	Public Affairs
SSA	Social Security Administration
UN	United Nations
UNDP	United Nations Development Program
UNESCO	United Nations Educational, Scientific and Cultural Organization

UNHCR	United Nations High Commissioner for Refugees
UNVIE	U.S. Mission to International Organizations in Vienna
USAF	U.S. Air Force
USAID	U.S. Agency for International Development
USDA	U.S. Department of Agriculture
USEU	U.S. Mission to the European Union
USIA	U.S. Information Agency (merged with State Department in 1999)
USIS	U.S. Information Service (USIA overseas, merged with State Dept. in 1999)
USTR	U.S. Trade Representative's Office
USUN	U.S. Mission to the United Nations
VA	Veterans Administration
VOA	Voice of America
WTO	World Trade Organization

Abbreviations for Embassy Positions

ADMIN	Administrative Officer
AGR	Agricultural Officer
AMB	Ambassador
CAO	Cultural Affairs Officer
CG	Consul General
CLO	Community Liaison Officer
COM	Commercial Officer
CONS	Consular Officer
DATT	Defense Attaché
DCM	Deputy Chief of Mission
DS	Diplomatic Security Officer
ECON	Economic Officer
EFM	Eligible Family Member
FSN	Foreign Service National
FSO	Foreign Service Officer
GSO	General Services Officer
IO	Information Officer
IMO	Information Management Officer
IMS	Information Management Specialist
JO	Junior Officer
LABATT	Labor Attaché
LEC	Law Enforcement Coordinator
MSG	Marine Security Guard
OMS	Office Management Specialist
PAO	Public Affairs Officer
POL	Political Officer
REO	Regional Environmental Officer
RMO	Regional Medical Officer
RSO	Regional Security Officer
USAID DIR	USAID Mission Director

Foreign Service and International Affairs Resources

American Foreign Service Association	www.afsa.org
U.S. Department of State	www.state.gov
Foreign Service Jobs	www.careers.state.gov
U.S. Agency for International Development	www.usaid.gov
U.S. Department of Agriculture	www.usda.gov
Foreign Agricultural Service	www.fas.usda.gov
U.S. Department of Commerce	www.commerce.gov
Foreign Commercial Service	www.usatrade.gov
International Broadcasting Bureau	www.ibb.gov
Peace Corps	www.peacecorps.gov
United States Embassies	usembassy.state.gov
Bureau of Diplomatic Security	ds.state.gov/index.html
North Atlantic Treaty Organization	www.nato.int
United Nations	www.un.org
European Union	europa.eu.int
Organization of American States	www.oas.org
Organization for Security and Cooperation in Europe	www.osce.org
World Bank	www.worldbank.org

American Academy of Diplomacy   www.academyofdiplomacy.org
A private, non-profit, non-partisan, elected society of
individuals who have held positions in the formulation
and implementation of American diplomacy.

American Diplomacy   www.unc.edu/depts/diplomat/
An electronic journal of commentary, analysis, and
research on American foreign policy and its practice.

Amnesty International   www.amnesty.org
A worldwide campaigning movement that works to
promote internationally recognized human rights.

Associates of the American Foreign Service Worldwide   www.aafsw.org
Information and resources for Foreign Service
family members.

Association of Diplomatic Studies and Training   www.adst.org
A private, non-profit organization that works to
advance understanding of U.S. diplomacy and supports
training of foreign affairs personnel.

Coalition for American Leadership Abroad   www.colead.org
A broad-based non-profit organization consisting
of over 30 member groups dedicated to furthering
well-informed public debate about international
issues affecting U.S. interests.

Foreign Affairs Magazine
A leading journal on international affairs and U.S. foreign policy, published by the Council on Foreign Relations.

www.foreignaffairs.org

Foreign Policy Association
Provides information on domestic and international issues, discussion groups, publications, events, etc.

www.fpa.org

Foreign Policy Magazine
A magazine of global politics, economics, and ideas.

www.foreignpolicy.com

Foreign Service Journal
A magazine for foreign affairs professionals, published by the American Foreign Service Association.

www.afsa.org/fsj

Foreign Service Youth Foundation
A non-profit organization providing information, outreach, and support for the internationally mobile families of U.S. Foreign Affairs agencies.

www.fsyf.org

InterAction
InterAction, the American Council for Voluntary Action, is a coalition of over 160 U.S.-based international development and humanitarian non-governmental organizations.

www.interaction.org

Public Diplomacy.org
Information regarding the role of public diplomacy in U.S. foreign policy.

www.publicdiplomacy.org

State Department Family Liaison Office
Working to improve the quality of life for Foreign Service families serving abroad by identifying problems and solutions in areas such as education, employment, and security.

www.state.gov/m/dghr/flo/

Tales From a Small Planet
This Web magazine started by Foreign Service family members seeks to share the experience of living abroad through literature, humor and the arts, and to provide information on what it's like to live in a foreign country. Site includes "Real Post Reports" — personal accounts of life in cities around the globe.

www.talesmag.com

U.S. Diplomatic History
The complete history of American foreign relations from the Declaration of Independence through the 1990s.

www.state.gov/history/

CIA World Factbook
Statistics and information on every country in the world. Includes flags and maps.

www.cia.gov/cia/publications/factbook/

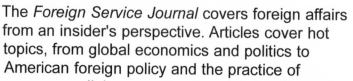

Inside a U.S. Embassy
www.afsa.org/inside

Please send _____ **copies of** *Inside a U.S. Embassy*
($12.95 per book plus shipping/handling) to:

Name: _____

Organization: _____

Address: _____

City: _____ State: _____ Zip: _____

Telephone: _____

E-mail: _____

To order by credit card:

Name on Card: _____

Type of Card: ☐ Visa ☐ MasterCard ☐ Discover ☐ American Express

Card Number: _____

Expiration date: _____

To order by mail, send payment and this form (or a purchase order) to:

Association Fulfillment Services
3030 Malmo Drive
Arlington Heights, IL 60005
Attn: Inside Embassy

Make check payable to American Foreign Service Association (or AFSA).

For shipping/handling costs, go to Purchase Book on the Web site, or call (847) 364-1222.

AFSA offers discounts on quantity orders. Visit the Web site for the discount list.

Send inquiries to embassybook@afsa.org or call AFSA at (202) 338-4045 or (800) 704-2372.

To order by phone, call (847) 364-1222, or fax (847) 364-1268.

To order online, go to www.afsa.org/inside and click on Purchase Book.

American Foreign Service Association
2101 E Street, N.W.
Washington, DC 20037
Telephone: (202) 338-4045 or (800) 704-2372
Fax: (202) 338-8244
E-mail: embassybook@afsa.org
Web site: www.afsa.org/inside